PUNISHMENT AND HUMAN RIGHTS

ISSUES IN CONTEMPORARY ETHICS
A Schenkman Series, Peter A. French, Editor

INDIVIDUAL AND COLLECTIVE RESPONSIBILITY
The Massacre at My Lai
 Edited by Peter A. French

THE MANSON MURDERS:
A Philosophical Inquiry
 Edited by David E. Cooper

CONSCIENTIOUS ACTIONS:
The Revelation of the Pentagon Papers
 Edited by Peter A. French

PUNISHMENT AND HUMAN RIGHTS
 Edited by Milton Goldinger

UTOPIA/DYSTOPIA?
 Edited by Peyton Richter

ASSASSINATION
 Edited by Harold Zellner

ABORTION
 Edited by Robert L. Perkins

PUNISHMENT AND HUMAN RIGHTS

Edited by Milton Goldinger

SCHENKMAN PUBLISHING COMPANY
Cambridge, Massachusetts

This book is distributed by
GENERAL LEARNING PRESS
250 James Street
Morristown, New Jersey 07960

Copyright © 1974
Schenkman Publishing Company
Cambridge, Massachusetts

Library of Congress Catalog Card Number: 74-78784
Printed in the United States of America

All rights reserved. This book, or parts thereof, may not be reproduced in any form without the written permission of the publishers.

CONTENTS

MILTON GOLDINGER
Introduction

Punishment and Morality:
the Basic Issues ... 1

SIDNEY GENDIN
A Critique of the Theory
of Criminal Rehabilitation ... 17

ANTONY FLEW
Delinquency and Mental Disease ... 39

MICHAEL D. BAYLES
Mental Abnormality
and the Criminal Process ... 57

T. L. S. SPRIGGE
Punishment and
Moral Responsibility ... 73

GERTRUDE EZORSKY
Punishment and Excuses ... 99

H. J. McCLOSKEY
The Morality of Punishment
of the "Moral" Criminal ... 117

HUGO ADAM BEDAU
A World Without Punishment? ... 141

BIBLIOGRAPHY ... 163

MILTON GOLDINGER

Introduction

Punishment and Morality: the Basic Issues

In the United States, a rising crime rate has produced a bitter emotional debate concerning the proper way to deal with criminals. One frequently voiced opinion, supported by a large segment of the general public, is that the best way to insure the public's safety is to "get tough" with the criminal by giving more severe sentences, decreasing the use of probation and parole, and ending the pampering of prisoners. Some opponents of this view, who often claim to possess a more "enlightened" attitude, consider the demand for severe punishments a vestige of barbarism, a needless and futile production of pain, or an emotional reaction stemming from the desire to get revenge. Rather than attempt to reduce crime by the threat of punishment, they maintain that our penal system should be directed towards treating the offender so that his criminal tendencies can be eliminated and he can be given a useful role in society.

To assess these and the numerous other positions on punishment, one must ignore the frequently impassioned rhetoric and examine both the empirical data and the moral principles which are used in their support. Although some of the differences regarding the proper role and value of punishment result from inadequate and conflicting empirical studies and data, not all differences can be traced to such causes. Some differences result either from disagreement on moral principles or from opposing views on the nature and extent of moral responsibility. The moral theories which have been most prominent in discussions of punishment and which produce many disputes current in our society are utilitarianism and retributivism. An understanding of these theories and their major variants will provide a sound basis for understanding the current disputes.

Punishment and Utility

The traditional utilitarian theory holds that acts productive of the greatest net good are right. Utilitarians differ regarding the states of affairs they consider good, but the good is usually equated with human happiness. In determining an act's rightness, only the goodness of the consequences is considered. Even acts of incest, murder, or infanticide, generally viewed by people with horror, are wrong only if they produce bad results. Although the traditional utilitarian is ultimately concerned with the rightness of particular acts, he recognizes the usefulness of requiring conformity to a system of laws. This conformity is thought to be obtainable by the use of various sanctions designed to make sure that illegal behavior is opposed to individual interest. Conformity to the law does not always produce the best results, however, so the laws are not sacrosanct and violations are not always wrong. But since respect for and adherence to the law is of great value to society, a heavy burden of proof rests on those who would support violations.

Acts of punishment, like other types of acts, are right if they produce as much good as possible. Many utilitarians maintain that the use of punishment is justified because it deters crime, isolates the criminal from society, aids in the criminal's reform, and satisfies society's desire for revenge. Deterrence is usually considered the most significant result offered by the use of punishment. Although some potential criminals cannot be deterred by the threat of punishment, such a threat can deter a number sufficiently large to justify its use. The threat of punishment is held to be an effective deterrent only insofar as the laws are adequately enforced and the social system is not so unjust that crime, for some, is a necessity. If the chances of escaping the punishment are high, or if the social system is such that men cannot satisfy basic wants without recourse to crime, then the deterrent effect of a system of punishments would be slight.

Many current debates regarding penal policies are conducted primarily within a utilitarian framework. Since any punishment causes harm to those who receive it, it is necessary for the utilitarian to show that the good results of punishment outweigh the harm produced. The debate over capital punishment, for example, often focuses on the question of its deterrent value. Advocates of such punishment claim that it is a valuable deterrent to certain crimes; opponents claim that there is no convincing evidence that it is any more effective than a long prison sentence and that, along with its other disadvantages, such punishment may even make it harder to get convictions in many cases. In advance of empirical evidence, utilitarians are not committed to any particular kinds of punishment for various crimes. If a three-year prison term deters murder as effectively as capital punishment or a life sentence, then the former is preferable since it causes less hardship to the criminal and generally less expense to society. Modifications in current penal policies would be required on utilitarian grounds if there were evidence to show that better results would be produced.

The utilitarian theory of punishment has often been criticized on moral grounds. Critics have argued that, under certain circumstances, the theory could result in the justification of acts which conflict with convictions generally held by rational, informed people about just treatment: punishment of an innocent person, punishment of those not responsible for their actions, and severe punishments for trivial crimes. The most frequently cited conflict with such moral convictions is the punishment of an innocent person. Although punishing an innocent person would usually not produce good results, it is possible to conceive of circumstances where it would. For example, suppose a leader of a foreign country is assassinated while visiting the United States. Unless the assassin is quickly apprehended and convicted, the foreign country will consider our government intolerably lax or even involved in the assassination; and serious problems, even a war, could result. Government leaders, having no knowledge of the real assassin, fabricate evidence which makes certain the conviction of a member of an anarchist organization. Convinced that they can keep the deceit a secret, they do not fear eventual exposure. The conviction would end any belief that the United States was involved in the assassination and so end tensions. Given such conditions (along with numerous others which could be specified) which insure the usefulness of the punishment, a utilitarian would deem the frame-up and conviction of the innocent anarchist morally right. Despite its utility, however, many would consider such undeserved punishment unacceptable.

Utilitarianism could also conflict with generally held convictions by justifying laws which allow punishment of those not responsible for their acts. Ordinarily such excuses as insanity, provocation, duress, mistake, and accident are held either to lessen or totally to eliminate responsibility; when no such excuse can be given, the offender is considered fully responsible. Since the knowledge that certain acts will be punished regardless of any excuse which can be given could make many people more cautious than they would be otherwise, laws disallowing various excuses could effectively prevent unintentional violations. In fact, our legal system now contains a number of such laws, termed strict liability laws, which are usually defended by reference to their value as a deterrent. For example, some states have laws requiring that tavern keepers be fined for selling alcohol to minors even if it is done unintentionally. It is thought that such laws will insure that tavern keepers will take great care to prevent such sales.

Underlying the objections to utilitarianism is the belief that any theory is unacceptable which justifies acts conflicting with moral convictions generally held by thoughtful, informed people. These convictions are treated by some theorists as basic data which a moral theory may clarify, systematize and make consistent, but not reject. W. D. Ross is typical of many who support the significance of such convictions.

> The existing body of moral convictions of the best people is the cumulative product of the moral reflection of many generations, which has developed an extremely delicate power of appreciation of moral distinctions; and this the theorist cannot afford to treat with anything other than the greatest respect. The verdicts of the moral consciousness of the best people are the foundation on which he must build; though he must first compare them with one another and eliminate any contradictions they may contain.[1]

By "best people" Ross is referring to the educated, thoughtful segment of the public. Compatibility with their convictions is, for him, the only defensible basis for establishing a moral position.

The demand that a moral theory be compatible with generally held moral convictions raises very complex issues. Some utilitarians have denied the need for a theory always to justify such convictions; to demand that it do so would enshrine current moral views. They argue that since the principle of utility, itself a deeply held moral conviction, provides a needed unitary basis for our judgments, it should be preferred to any conflicting conviction which is no more strongly held. Opponents agree that the principle of utility is a strongly held conviction, but they maintain that some incompatible convictions are even more strongly held. They claim, for example, that few people would consider the punishment of an innocent person justified even though it produced better results than any other action would.

Some utilitarians have argued that, even if generally held convictions are admitted to be of some significance, it is arguable whether actions conflicting with them must always be considered wrong. Such convictions are believed to have gained an imposing status with theorists primarily because they usually reflect the utility of various actions in ordinary circumstances. They have developed out of mankind's experiences with various actions and are indicative of what is generally useful. There is no reason for believing that their wide acceptance rests on any intuitive basis or any special moral sense. Generally held convictions may be an important guide to the usefulness of various acts, but these convictions have not developed in response to unusual circumstances and they can give no guidance, even about utility, in such circumstances.

Despite the uncertainty about the significance of generally held convictions, many contemporary utilitarians contend that their theory must not justify acts that conflict with such convictions, even in unusual circumstances. In part, this contention is due to the fact that utilitarians believe their own theory can be established only by its acceptability to reasonable, informed people. If, even in unusual circumstances, acts justified on utilitarian grounds are, after careful consideration, deemed morally unacceptable, then the theory would be indefensible. The realization that their theory could apparently justify acts that conflict with strongly held convictions has led many utilitarians to support a modification of their theory which would eliminate, or at least greatly reduce, possible conflicts.

The most important attempt to modify utilitarianism in order to avoid conflicts with our accepted moral convictions is rule utilitarianism. According to this theory, rather than perform those acts which produce the most good, one should follow rules which, if generally followed, would produce the best results. Particular acts are right only if they are stipulated by the set of rules which are justified on utilitarian grounds. When applied to punishment, this theory maintains that individual acts of punishment must be specified by the rules or laws of a defensible penal system. Another way this theory's position on punishment is explained is in terms of the various roles or tasks one has within an institution. In our penal system, the legislator has the task of making the laws, and the judge has the task of making decisions by reference to those laws. Because of their assigned role, judges cannot decide individual cases in a manner which they believe would promote society's welfare; they must make their decisions within the limits set by the law. It is only the legislator in framing laws who can base his decisions directly on the principle of utility. Such a modification of utilitarianism is held to make much more unlikely than the traditional view the justification of punishing an innocent man since such punishment would have to be allowable by a law. Presumably any law which allowed punishment of the innocent would so frighten a large segment of the public that it would be highly unlikely to produce good results.

Although this version of utilitarianism is perhaps less likely to justify unjust treatment than the traditional version, this would not satisfy those who maintain that an acceptable theory must never justify such treatment. The difficulty for the rule utilitarian is that the rules which are justifiable on utilitarian grounds do not insure that all those liable to punishment as a result of a breach of the law will be, in any usual sense of the term, deserving. The rule utilitarian could, especially if the crime rate increased alarmingly or in other unusual circumstances, justify laws requiring the punishment of all offenders regardless of their responsibility, punishment of a criminal's family, or severe penalties for minor crimes. For example, with our usual penalties against such acts, suppose it were found to be extremely difficult to prevent government and military personnel from giving military secrets vital to the nation's defense to the enemy for economic gain. A law requiring torture and imprisonment of a traitor's family could reduce the number of traitorous acts. Despite the increased insecurity of many innocent families, the overall effects of the law would be judged good. If so, the law would have to be approved on rule utilitarian grounds. Since such a law specifies punishments for innocent people, the theory, by justifying the law, conflicts with the conviction that only those responsible for crimes should be punished. Thus, this version of the theory, like the traditional variety, would be considered morally objectionable.

Punishment as Retribution

The retributive theory of punishment, the most important alternative to the utilitarian theory, holds that the consequences of punishment are irrelevant for its moral assessment; only considerations of moral desert are appropriate in determining its justification. Punishment must be given in response to the misdeeds for which the criminal is responsible and must fit the crime. Concern with the criminal's desert requires that the penal system be designed so that punishment is given to all and only those who are responsible for an offense, and the punishment's severity must be proportionate to the gravity of the crime. For most retributivists, one can be responsible for a criminal act only if the act could have been known to be criminal when committed and a different act was capable of being performed. The former condition would eliminate any responsibility for performing an act which later became an offense (*ex post facto* laws), and the latter would eliminate responsibility for those who act under duress, while insane or incompetent, or due to mistakes or ignorance.

The retributive theory is often supported on the ground that it is more in accord with generally held views of justice than is utilitarianism. Since retributivism restricts punishment to those responsible for crimes, it precludes any possible justification of punishing an innocent person; and since it requires that the severity of a punishment be proportionate to the gravity of a crime, it precludes the possibility of overpunishment. For the retributivist, a person deserving a particular punishment must receive it, nothing more or less: the punishment cannot be increased or lessened to help either the criminal or society. Insofar as mercy involves giving the criminal less than the deserved penalty, the retributivist would consider it unjustifiable. He is not opposed to the reduction or elimination of punishment because of various mitigating or excusing factors, however, since this does not involve mercy but merely the adjustment of the penalty in order to achieve the deserved result.

In this traditional form, retributivism leads to results that are as discordant with generally held convictions as those derived from utilitarianism. This stems from the fact that the retributive theory does not allow for any modification of a just penalty. The meting out of deserved penalties without concern for mercy or social welfare seems uncomfortably restrictive. For example, consider a first offender, convicted of only a minor crime, who can continue to support his family if he receives a suspended sentence. A thirty day sentence for his crime will cause social and economic hardships for his family. Though he is responsible for his crime and deserves punishment, many people would feel that he should be given a "second chance" for the sake of his family. For the retributivist, the welfare of the family would be an irrelevant consideration in deciding whether to punish.

Because of such difficulties, some present-day theorists have supported a modified version of retributivism. Like traditional retributivists, modern retributivists hold that punishment must be given only to those responsible for offenses and that such punishment must be no greater than the criminal deserves; unlike traditional retributivists, they hold that considerations of justice give the right but not the obligation to punish. Since deserved penalties are not obligatory, they can be remitted or lessened to produce good results. One strength of this modern version is that it allows for the possibility of mercy. Since in many cases both the retributively proper penalty and a lesser penalty will be equally permissible, the choice of the lesser, merciful penalty is a possibility.

The modern retributivist theory, like others we have examined, is not without difficulties. One difficulty results from the fact that the theory does not produce any obligations regarding the application of punishment. Insofar as both the retributively just penalty and a lesser, more useful penalty are equally right, there would appear to be no moral basis by means of which a decision between them could be made. Thus, if a legislative assembly always framed laws that required the imposition of the most severe penalty permissible or a judge always imposed the most severe punishment allowable by law, there would be no moral basis for complaint even though an equally permissible, less severe penalty would produce better results. The decision to give the harsher, but equally just penalty, could not be objected to on moral grounds since there is no obligation to choose one permissible penalty even though it produces the best results. It is not open to the modern retributivists to maintain that of two right penalties the one productive of the best results should be chosen, for this would produce definite obligations and thus eliminate that which they conceive to be essential for mercy: the freedom to choose among various right penalties.

Besides the various divergencies from common moral convictions cited for each version of retributivism, both views are confronted with the difficult task of explaining how to proportion the severity of the punishment to the gravity of the crime.[2] Both versions must determine the appropriate amount of punishment for various crimes; the traditional retributivist to give that amount and the modern retributivist to know the permissible limits. Possible means of assessing the gravity of a crime are the actual harm done and the motives of the agent.

Any contention that punishment should be proportioned to the actual harm done is faced with serious difficulties. Such a view would have to reject the kinds of excuses that are ordinarily accepted as sufficient to mitigate or eliminate the culpability of the agent. Further, according to this view there would seem to be no satisfactory way of handling group crimes. How much should each of six men be punished who are convicted of a single murder? To give all six death or a life sentence would be, for this approach, overpunishment; in fact, were one given such a penalty, the other should be freed, for the appropriate amount of reciprocal harm apparently would have been produced.

If the gravity of a crime is assessed on the basis of the motives of the agent, there must be a means of ranking motives by their degree of badness and of determining how much punishment is deserved for acts that stem from various motives. Besides the obvious fact that we have no means of making such determinations, several disconcerting consequences would follow from a reliance on motives. If motives alone determine the gravity of a crime, then all crimes that result from the same motive should be punished equally, regardless of the harm caused. Another consequence of such a view is that it would seem impossible to justify punishing anyone who broke the law as a result of morally admirable motives. If such people were exempt from punishment, the legal system would be powerless to protect the public from ignorant but well meaning people.

The Rejection of Punishment

So far we have been considering the justifications offered for the use of punishment. Currently, a growing number of theorists contend that punishment is either ineffective as a deterrent or that it is unjust and should be replaced with nonpunitive measures designed to reform the offender. This view, the reform theory, should not be confused with a view that supports the use of punishment as a means to reform criminal offenders. Reform theorists desire to bring about in an offender a disposition to keep within the law by means other than by fear of punishment and to help the offender become a productive member of society. They do not want merely to use for rehabilitative treatment the time a criminal is incarcerated, but to substitute for traditional punitive measures such nonpunitive ones as psychiatric therapy, vocational training, halfway houses, indeterminate sentences, and early paroles. Incarceration, sometimes necessary to insure that the criminal will receive treatment and to protect the public until it is completed, is never used for a deterrent or punitive effect.

The justification offered for the reform theory is often a utilitarian one. It is contended that the threat of punishment has little deterrent effect upon potential criminals and that those who actually receive punishment often commit further crimes upon their release from prison. Replacement of the traditional prison system, which degrades the criminal and often increases the likelihood that he will commit future crimes, with a system which rehabilitates would have a number of valuable results. It would lower the rate of recidivism and thereby reduce the overall crime rate. It would be beneficial to the criminal since it would eliminate the punishment he would ordinarily receive and prepare him for a satisfactory life. Finally, society would gain not only by the reduced rate of recidivism but by the increase in the number of law-abiding and productive citizens.

Certainly, the empirical claims made regarding the ineffectiveness of punishment as a deterrent and the effectiveness of nonpunitive treatment in reducing recidivism and aiding the criminal need a great deal of supporting evidence; but, at the present time, the necessary evidence is unavailable. Not only have attempts to reform criminals not been particularly successful, but claims regarding the ineffectiveness of punishment as a deterrent are difficult to substantiate. A high crime rate in a country with a penal system designed to deter does not necessarily indicate the failure of such a system; the crime rate might be due to poor enforcement or a grossly unjust social system. Rectifying such defects and maintaining a deterrent system of punishments might produce better results than the adoption of the reformist program. Finally, it is not clear that a reformist program could do one of the jobs that utilitarians believe necessary, namely, deterring potential offenders. The reformists aim their measures solely at those who have committed crimes, but do not provide any measures designed to dissuade ordinary citizens from becoming offenders, particularly if the reform program works as designed, that is, actually reforms the criminal and returns him to a useful place in society without any stigma. At the present time the program of treatment is often long and the offender's prospects are not enhanced by his criminal record. If, however, the treatment given for various crimes were not long and the individual's future prospects would not be harmed by a criminal record, many might feel that the possible gain from the commission of a crime would be worth the risked inconvenience of therapy. If, for example, a man knows that for killing his wife he will likely receive six to twelve months treatment in a mental hospital, then he might decide that the treatment is preferable to living with a shrewish wife or paying her alimony.

A very different argument for the reformist position is based on some widely disputed views of moral responsibility and the causes of criminal behavior. This argument may be stated as follows:

1. Criminals are incapable of acting other than they do.
2. Those incapable of acting other than they do are not responsible for their crimes.

Therefore, criminals are not responsible for their crimes.

3. Those not responsible for their crimes should not be punished.

Therefore, criminals should not be punished for their crimes.

4. Those who should not be punished for their crimes should be rehabilitated.

Therefore, criminals should be rehabilitated.

The argument is valid. Since the conclusions will be true if the premises are true, we must examine the reasons reformists have given for accepting the premises.

Premise (1) has been defended on the basis of either of two often disputed contentions: that man's behavior is determined or that crime is the result of mental illness. Many famous reformists, such as Robert Owen and Clarence Darrow, have argued for the truth of (1) on the basis of a belief in determinism, i.e., the belief that all events are the result of prior causes. Generally conjoined with the belief in universal causation is the claim that events occur in orderly patterns which can be formulated as causal or natural laws. Knowledge of these laws and of existing states of affairs would make all future events predictable. Human actions are as predictable as any other event; such predictability eliminates any possibility that one's actions could have been other than they were. Determinists believe that the actual inability to predict much of human behavior results not from any indeterminism in the universe but from our present insufficient knowledge of causal laws.

Reformists with training or interest in psychology frequently support (1) on the basis of the claim that criminal conduct is the result of mental illness. Crime is never viewed by these theorists as resulting from a rational choice but from mental disease which, if properly treated, can be cured. Such a view is open to serious objections. To establish the truth of (1), it must be shown not only that criminal acts result from some kind of mental illness, but also that the illness is such that it takes away the capacity to control one's behavior or to know what one is doing. Certain types of crimes, such as child molestation, may result from a requisite type of mental illness, but, at present, there is little evidence to indicate that all criminal actions result from some type of compulsive behavior or insanity. Many forgers, embezzlers, and tax evaders certainly appear to act on the basis of an assessment of their chances for economic gain. The inability to specify the nature of many criminals' illnesses has led some reformists to contend that criminal conduct is itself evidence of mental illness. Such a contention, however, begs the question. To point out that they committed crimes is not sufficient to establish that criminals are ill or could not have avoided committing their crimes. Criminal behavior can be used as evidence of mental illness only if it is established that crimes are caused by such illnesses.

Premise (2) asserts that causally determined behavior and moral responsibility are incompatible. As stated above, it is a widely held view that people are not responsible for acts which they could not avoid. Given this view, determinism, which denies the possibility that actions could be other than they are, would eliminate any moral responsibility. Clarence Darrow is typical of those reformists who have maintained the incompatibility of moral responsibility and determinism.

> Man is in no sense the maker of himself and has no more power than any machine to escape the law of cause and effect. He does what he must.

Therefore, there is no such thing as moral responsibility in the sense in which the expression is ordinarily used.[3]

In many of his well-known trials, Darrow based his client's defense on the contention that the world is determined and that in such a world the criminal is not responsible. His famous defense of Leopold and Loeb, for example, was made on such a basis. Darrow argued that various hereditary and environmental factors had prevented his defendants from developing normal emotional reactions, and so they should be pitied for their crime, not blamed.

Some theorists, often labeled soft-determinists, deny that determinism and moral responsibility are incompatible. These theorists claim that the fact that an individual's act was caused is irrelevant for assessing moral responsibility. One reason given for this view is that moral responsibility for an act requires only that the act be free; and, according to ordinary and legal usage, an act is free if it is neither compelled by external forces nor the result of internal compulsion. Ordinarily, choices and decisions that are the result, say, of childhood upbringing and other environmental influences, are not considered compelled. A man's decision to go into his father's business or to steal is considered free if there were no unusual forces or constraints producing the decision. Moral responsibility, then, requires only that acts be uncompelled, not uncaused. The correctness of the soft-determinist view hinges on an assessment of the ordinary conception of a free act. The soft-determinist could be correct about the way the notion of a free action is ordinarily conceived, but this conception might not take into account the full implications of determinism.

Premise (3) makes a moral claim which can be argued for on either utilitarian or modern retributivist grounds. We have already seen, however, that a utilitarian defense of this claim is confronted with serious difficulties. Utilitarians have often tried to show that their theory would not result in justifying punishment of those who are not responsible, but they are unable to refute the claim that their theory could lead to the justification of laws which allowed the punishment of those who are not responsible if such laws would have the greatest utility. A stronger defense of (3) can be made on modern retributivist grounds. Premise (3) could also, of course, be defended on traditional retributivist grounds; but, given the defense that the reformist must make of (4), it will be seen that the modern version is the only plausible one for the reformist to adopt. It should be recalled that for the modern retributivist punishment must be deserved to be justified.

A criminal's lack of responsibility would eliminate any ill-desert and thus make any punishment unjustified.

Even if the reformist can establish that criminals should not be punished, he must still show that the reform program is justified. Premise (4), which asserts the correctness of reforming those who should not be punished, can be given, as can premise (3), a modern retributivist defense. The modern retributivist allows criminals to be treated in ways that are beneficial to them and society insofar as the requirements of justice are not violated. Thus, after establishing the injustice of punishment, reformation appears to be the only acceptable way of dealing with criminals. An attempt to reform criminals seems preferable to wholly ignoring their crimes. Defending reform on such a basis must seem odd to those who have always thought of retribution as involving vengeance or harsh penalties. Yet, given the reformist argument, such a defense certainly can be justified. Modern retributivists have rarely emphasized the compatibility of their position with reform because they generally reject the truth of (1).

Besides the difficulties that can be raised regarding the premises of this argument, reformists have been attacked on the ground that their program leads to morally unacceptable results. Difficulties arise because of the reformist's espousal of the indeterminate sentence in conjunction with a therapeutic program. With no limit placed on the time an offender can be forced to undergo treatment, those who either respond to treatment slowly or do not respond at all could remain incarcerated for great lengths of time. This possibility is especially disturbing since it could befall those who have committed very minor offenses and who would ordinarily receive a small fine or a few weeks in jail. Such offenders might be kept confined and subject to therapy indefinitely. This possible result is unsatisfactory on two counts. First, the harm to the offender is greater than any benefit derived by the community. Second, it violates the requirement that trivial crimes not be given severe penalties. The reformist might object here that treatment is not a penalty. Nonetheless, since the treatment can be lengthy and undesired, one should not be forced to suffer it for a minor offense. Concern for justice would require that an appropriate upper limit be placed on any penalty or treatment for a criminal offense. This, of course, would necessitate releasing the offender after he served the appropriate time regardless of the success of his rehabilitation.

Still another problem for the reformist arises with regard to the application of his theory to groups of criminals who do not appear to be in need of rehabilitation. Those who commit illegal acts to protest what they conceive to be unconscionable laws or those who refuse induction into the military to fight what they believe to be an unjust war would be examples. For the government to force treatment upon such people could be to use the reform program to insure acceptance of the society's or government's moral and political views. Although a government might be justified in punishing those who because of moral disagreement break laws, it does not seem justified in forcing offenders by means of various therapeutic devices to accept its views.

The foregoing account of some of the main problems involved in the moral assessment of punishment neither includes all the major problems nor exhausts the possible approaches that might be taken to solve them. It should, however, provide the readers of this volume with a framework for critically appraising the papers that follow, each of which provides original and detailed analyses of one or more of the issues touched on here. Although the authors by no means concur in their moral stands or in their analyses of particular issues, they all present reasoned defenses of their views. It is hoped that a careful assessment of their arguments will provide both a greater understanding of the complexity of the problems and a basis for their solution.

NOTES

[1] W. D. Ross, *The Right and the Good* (Oxford: The Clarendon Press, 1930), p. 41.

[2] For a detailed discussion of this difficulty, see Richard Brandt, *Ethical Theory* (Englewood Cliffs, N.J.: Prentice-Hall, Inc., 1959), pp. 462-464.

[3] Clarence Darrow, *Crime: Its Cause and Treatment* (New York: Thomas Y. Crowell Company, 1922), pp. 274-275.

SIDNEY GENDIN

A Critique of the Theory of Criminal Rehabilitation

"We have a more magnificent idea of objects in proportion as they are less familiar." Jeremy Bentham

Nowadays almost no one dares question the idea of criminal rehabilitation as the proper goal of penology. Punishment is said to be wasteful of our time and resources, futile as a means of checking criminal conduct, and outright barbaric. It is a fact of life, unfortunately, that at most penetentiaries more than half the prison populations are made up of repeaters. Surely, most criminologists argue, if we are to make headway against crime it is not enough to punish a person for his past misdeeds. We must make him over into a person less likely to commit a criminal act again.

The above argument is so high-minded and humane-sounding that one feels almost villainous for criticizing it. Yet one must. For only insofar as the idea of rehabilitation is not fully comprehended will we be tempted to give it our unswerving admiration.

Rehabilitation, Humanitarianism, and Some Muddles

Clearly no one objects in and of itself to the rehabilitation of a criminal. Wherever rehabilitation is feasible, everyone of good will must welcome it wholeheartedly. The catch, of course, is what is meant by "feasible." This should be understood to mean not merely "practically possible and worth attempting" but also "intelligible and coherent." The dismal truth is that we have no single notion as to what rehabilitation is and only obscure ideas concerning how any of the competing goals of rehabilitation are to be achieved. But even if we should succeed in working out a systematic theory, there is already good reason to think that rehabilitation has a very limited range of application, and that at best it could serve only as an adjunct to punishment and not as a thoroughgoing replacement of it.

To begin with, we need to distinguish only briefly between the Rehabilitation Theory and the Reform Theory of Punishment. According to the latter, punishment is justified, but not for any retributive reason or for its deterrence value. Rather, it is good for the man who receives it because it improves his character. This view is a very old one. Plato, for instance, presented it in several of his dialogues. It is true that sometimes the intensity of society's response to someone's wrong act may impress strongly on that person how much society cares. In that sense the pain of punishment may be educative. For the most part, however, law-breakers already know how much society cares — witness the precautions they take against getting caught. The pains of punishment are more usually viewed by the criminal as vengeance being wreaked upon him. He will hardly consider the punishment as doing him any good. And that *he* doesn't think it is doing him any good is important, for if punishment builds resentments and deepens hostilities then it has no chance of bringing about reformation. I am inclined to think that if any improvement is made in a prisoner's character it comes from the extra-punitive measures that are taken during his stay in prison and not from the imprisonment itself. Once we contrast reformation *through* punishment with rehabilitation *instead of* punishment, I don't think there would be many serious advocates of the former. In any case, I propose to say no more about it.

Apart from contrasting it with reformation, we have not yet given any account of rehabilitation. Nor is it easy to do so. One good reason for this is that most talk about rehabilitation is really only meta-rehabilitation talk. We are not really told, if we read the rehabilitation tracts, how rehabilitation is accomplished. Rather, we are told why it should be pursued or how to ready ourselves for doing rehabilitory work. Thus one writer presents what he calls "thesis" about rehabilitation, and his first and "primary theses" reads:

> It is essential that our citizens in general participate in the treatment of criminals. By this I mean that the correctional system must not continue to be a restricted area to which only officials have access.[1]

Now this is a well-intentional combination of pronouncements that is hard to resist, and I, for one, happen to agree with the second part. But to state this as "a primary thesis" of rehabilitation rather than as an incidental, albeit important, remark about attitudes toward rehabilitation is curious in the extreme. Nor are we given any account of what it is that citizens are supposed to do when participating in treatment. What "rehabilitation" the author does specify is not of criminals but of the public. Thus, when citizens participate in treatment, "there is no better way of correcting misconceptions and dispelling the mystique surrounding crime."[2] Their role is to play "a part in informing the public . . . about the true nature of criminals."[3] In other words, to a very large extent, "rehabilitation" consists in getting the public to maintain a well-disposed attitude towards ex-convicts. Plainly, an ex-convict makes a better adjustment to society if he does not have to confront prejudice and unfair treatment at every turn. And just as plainly, this doesn't prove a single thing about rehabilitation. But notice that even this kind of "rehabilitation" is only held out to us as a promise. It is not the promise that some method will produce good results but the expression of a faith —a faith that, if people will observe prison inmates for themselves, their bigotry will wither away. Whether this is true or not, this is not the faith of a person who believes in the possibility of rehabilitation but rather the faith of one who believes rehabilitation is unnecessary.

Rehabilitation procedures are often confused with humanitarian procedures. That is, the latter are taken for the former. Penetentiaries were once little more than hellholes. Every man sent to one was bound to be punished disproportionately to his offense. Consider what one prisoner has written:

> One of the minor curiosities of jail life was that they quickly provided you with a hundred worries which left you no time or energy for worrying about your sentence, long or short . . . rather as if you were thrown into a fire with spikes in it, and the spikes hurt so much that you forgot about the fire. But then your punishment would be the spikes and not the fire. Why did they pretend it was only the fire, when they knew very well about the spikes?[4]

Today, instead of a damp cell lit by a single dim bulb, with a barred window too high to look through, a prisoner may have a well ventilated room with adequate lighting and a window that is really a window. Food is no longer necessarily "institutional food," and insanely striped uniforms meant to be degrading are now passé. There is pay for work, less crowding, better libraries, better recreational facilities and, in some of the more experimental prisons, even facilities for conjugal visitations.

All these are welcome changes. But none of these improvements bear on the theory of punishment or on the theory of rehabilitation. For if we take seriously, as we should, the idea that one is sentenced to prison *as* a punishment rather than *for* punishment, then we need not think of these improvements as signifying the end of punishment or as molly-coddling. As Mabbott points out, men are not sentenced to starvation, brutality or pneumonia; a man gets his deserved punishment when he is imprisoned for the appropriate length of time.[5] The danger, however, in adopting these improvements lies in this: if we think of their justification in terms of their rehabilitative effects, then what if they fail to rehabilitate? We will have undermined our grounds for having adopted them. Measures that ought to have been adopted in any event run the risk of being dropped in frustration. And, indeed, we must own up now to the distinction between the humane handling of prisoners for its own sake and such handling in the hope that in some vague way good consequences will come about; for the failure of humane handling as a tool of rehabilitation has already been documented:

> The bleak fact is that just as the monstrous punishments of the eighteenth century failed to curtail crime, so the more humane handling of the twentieth century has equally failed to do so.[6]

It has even been said that the most significant innovation in rehabilitation during the last hundred years is the use of the suspended sentence. But how can refraining from punishment be rehabilitative? Surely it is closer to the truth to say that, in most cases where suspended sentences are given, the reason for suspending sentence is that in the court's opinion no good purpose would be served by putting the person behind bars. He is viewed as one "who made a mistake any one might make" or as "someone who deserves another chance." In short, he is seen as a person who does not seem to be in need of rehabilitation. This is a matter of humanitarian enlightenment. To view the suspended sentence as an instance of, or even as part of, his rehabilitation is a fallacy.

Crimes *Mala In Se* and *Mala Prohibita*

Prior to the questions of why people commit crimes and of what can be done to rehabilitate them is the question — "What is crime?" One's answer is bound to influence one's view about the morality and the very intelligibility of rehabilitation as *the* goal of penology. There are conflicting ideas on this topic. For example, there is the distinction between *malum in se* and *malum prohibitum*. This may be regarded as the distinction only between what is wrong in itself and what is wrong because specifically prohibited by law. But Black's Law Dictionary also calls *malum in se* "an act or case involving *illegality* from the very nature of the transaction." (My italics) This definition encourages the idea of crime as part of the objective order of things. By contrast, there is the equally time-honored principle *nulla poena sine lege*. Indeed, the repugnance we feel towards *ex post facto* laws is that they violate the latter principle.

Our objection to *ex post facto* laws is not easily, if at all, accountable for on the basis of a pure rehabilitation theory.[7] Most rehabilitationists think of crime not as the reason for our intervention but merely as the occasion which spurs us on to intervention. As Karpmann, a leading spokesman for rehabilitation, puts it, "Basically, criminality is but a symptom of insanity." If one looks at the matter this way, one may be inclined to feel that there is no special merit in waiting for the outbreak of symptoms before treating the underlying malady. Anyone who is "discovered" to have the "potential" for criminal behavior is as rightly treated as one who has committed a crime. However, if we accept this medical model, there is no good reason why we should even wait until we stumble over these discoveries. Periodic examinations of all persons are quite in order. This concept is reinforced by the idea that crime is not only an illness, but a highly infectious "social disease." Since at least the time of Ferri, rehabilitationists have resorted to disease metaphors when describing what they call the "course" of criminality. A recent description goes like this:

> Using medical terms, delinquency can be described as a very widespread illness, affecting mainly young people and causing gross symptoms . . . Mild cases are usually treated at home . . . The illness on the whole is benign. Unfortunately (in some cases, after recovery) it is followed by relapses. The illness then takes a prolonged course . . .[8]

Once we look at the matter in this way, procedural safeguards become unimportant. The notion of *burden of proof* gives way to the notion of *best available diagnosis,* and worries about the injustice of a diagnosis and indeterminacy of treatment seem as out of place as they would be for physically ill people. Principles of justice lose their intelligibility within the framework of a pure rehabilitative theory.[9]

Most rehabilitationists accept the idea that crimes are part of the objective order of things and do not have to be declared as such in a legal system. But some strange twists in the rehabilitation theory are required to account for certain facts. Consider the fact, for example, that in one typical year — 1912 — 106,000 arrests were made in Chicago for acts that had not been offenses twenty years earlier. A rehabilitationist, with his attention riveted on such acts as murder, rape, and robbery, might say that those who had committed those same acts in 1892 were just as criminaly minded as those who committed them in 1912. It is understandable that the more dramatic crimes should be the ones that treatment specialists have in mind when they think about crime. But this narrow focusing causes one to overlook the fact that among the acts one may have done with impunity in 1892 but not in 1912 were such things as: keeping a store open on a Sunday; keeping a wild animal as a pet; shooting a deer in August; peddling merchandise without a license; and transporting a dead body without a permit.

Of course, an extreme advocate of the view that crime is evidence of disease might say that, if an act is legal when it is done, then doing it is not evidence of disease; but, when the act is illegal, then it is evidence. It is perhaps from this standpoint that we should view J. R. Rees's remark:

> *All* failure to comply with the rules of *the game* . . . is evidence of some psychological failure in the conduct of life.[10] (My italics)

Notice how this changes the character of the "psychological failure" thesis. It is no longer the nature of the act that points to the need for rehabilitation. *Any* act can indicate mental illness if it is contrary to law. We may say that according to this view it is lawbreaking which is the sickness. Now, indeed, a person who will break the law just in order to break the law seems quite a queer sort. But the suggestion that most criminals are motivated by a desire to break "the rules of the game" is too farfetched to waste time on. Hopefully, few psychiatrists subscribe to this theory[11]

The Kinds and Numbers of Crimes There Are

Consider the following enumeration of real and possible crimes, consisting of misdemeanors and felonies, but arranged in a (nearly) random way:

1. A woman burns draft records as part of a war protest.
2. A physician performs an abortion illegal in his state.
3. A person flies a kite in an area restricted to balloons.
4. Because he knows for certain that his friend is innocent of a crime of which he is accused, a person perjures himself to provide an alibi.
5. A driver commits a hit-and-run.
6. A professor sells his used textbooks but does not report the sales as income.
7. Late at night, having to relieve himself but with no facilities about, a person urinates against a building wall — observed only by the arresting officer.
8. A foreign agent is arrested for spying.
9. F.B.I. agents engage in unauthorized wiretapping.
10. A person who was uninjured in an automobile accident sues for $20,000, claiming whiplash injury.
11. To preserve the promised anonymity of his interviewees, the chairman of a commission to investigate prison riots destroys his files rather than surrender them when they are subpoenaed.
12. A woman lies above a man in sexual embrace, thereby committing "an unnatural act."
13. Noticing that the cashier has given him back far too much change, a man quickly pockets it all.
14. A man's store is robbed. He can identify the culprit but, from fear, refuses to do so.
15. A group of young men are guilty of "breaking and entering" when they climb over a school yard fence to play softball.
16. A person prepares documents and advises persons on how to obtain a divorce and is thereby guilty of unlicensed practice of law.
17. A psychiatrist who is the Chief of Rehabilitation Services at a large modern prison murders his wife.

In this variegated list one is hard put to find a unifying theme. One may be appalled to find some acts illegal; in other cases, provided that the penalties are trivial enough, one will be amused. Still other acts properly outrage most people. Some of these acts may seem to be *mala in se* while others seem to be *mala prohibita*. Nor can one presume that an offense is a serious one because it belongs among the former or that it is not serious because it belongs among the latter. I shall not defend the propriety or impropriety of the inclusion of any or all of these acts on a list of offenses. Instead, I call attention to two things: (1) If one pays attention to the totality of acts that are offenses (whether on the above list or not) in this or any other country, one will notice that the "classic" crimes — murder, rape, robbery, etc. — make up not only a small proportion of the *kinds* of crimes but a small proportion of the total *number* of crimes that are committed daily. (2) More arguably, perhaps, I would say that a unifying theme among all the crimes in the above list is that none indicates that the offender needs rehabilitation. Indeed, most of these crimes are of such a nature that we are at a loss to imagine just what it is that a treatment specialist is supposed to do.

A few persons have suggested to me that it is logically possible that a person arrested, say, for flying a kite in an area restricted to balloon-flying might never do this again if he were given shock therapy. Or perhaps some imaginative new surgical operation would produce this result. I do not deny it, and can go even further. It is logically possible that if I eat a tomato one Saturday afternoon a certain kite-flyer one thousand miles away will never fly his kite in a balloon area again. But such flights of fancy seem to me to prove nothing because they prove too much. Appeals to sheer logical possibility seem to be appeals to stop philosophizing. I am trying to show that there is something absurd in the idea that every crime indicates the need for rehabilitation, and simply to be told that it is logically possible that one who commits a crime of a sort I am discussing might never commit it again if something were done to him strikes me as true, but boring. And it presents no challenge to my claim that talk of rehabilitation in that case is absurd.

I want to make one more point about this "challenge" based on logical possibilities. It is evident, I think, that not everything that is a crime ought to be a crime. If, say, abortion should not be illegal, then the idea of "curing" or "rehabilitating" a fully qualified physician who performs an abortion is a confused idea. I am not denying the logical possibility that something can be done to the physician so that he will never want to perform an abortion again. But not every change is a cure. Geach points out in *Mental Acts* that if a boy came to know Latin by submitting to a brain operation, he still would not have *learned* Latin. Not every case of coming-to-know is a case of learning. Likewise, not every case of getting-a-man-to-cease-and-desist is a case of rehabilitating him.

The Notion of "Real Crime"

Some criminologists recognize that the question "What is a crime?" has, logically, to precede the question "How do we rehabilitate a person who commits a crime?" But their enthusiasm for approaching first things first sometimes has a faulty basis. One such faulty basis is the belief that a person who commits a "real crime" is not merely a person who does some thing wrong or who violates a law but is someone who is a "criminal." "Lawbreaker" and "criminal" are not synonymous either in the popular conception or in the minds of professionals. Thus, criminologists use a classifcation called "occasional offender" which is exclusive of the classification "criminal type." A person is a criminal type only if he habitually commits *real* crimes. A professor who regularly chooses not to report the sale of used books as income does not thereby gain entry into the class of habitual criminals because he is not committing the "right kind" of crime. Hence, lurking behind the asking of the question "What is a crime?" is usually the desire to identify "real criminal types" — i.e., just those whom criminologists hope to impress on us as good candidates for rehabilitation.[12]

We need not deny that many persons are criminals because of certain traits they share. Perhaps these are psychological defects or learned antisocial habits common in certain subcultures. Perhaps most criminals who commit robberies and burglaries do so because they lack the vocational and educational skills needed to earn honest livings. It could be granted, for the sake of argument, that all criminals are of the above sorts. But if the rehabilitation theory is something more than the claim that rehabilitation *just contingently happens to be* the best way to handle all offenders, it must be shown that it is impossible for normal, well-educated, and highly skilled people to commit crimes. For if it is not impossible, the question arises, "What should be done if such a person commits a crime?". *Ex hypothesi,* he is not a candidate for rehabilitation. Should he be punished? This is a moral question that cannot be answered merely by ascertaining that the person does not need rehabilitation. If all we have is a theory about what to do with persons needing rehabilitation, then, no matter how good that theory, it is of no use to us when we need to know what to do with persons not in need of rehabilitation.

Those who are concerned with developing the idea of real crime are probably unduly sanguine about the possibility of influencing legislative bodies. Even supposing a theoretically satisfactory answer to the question "What is crime?" can be given, there still is no particularly good reason to think that, in practice, only that which conformed to the theoretically satisfactory definition would be regarded as a crime. The majority of our laws reflect the desires and needs of special interest groups, and there is every reason to suppose that these groups would continue to lobby and work in other ways for their pet laws. For example, some people insist that the private possession of guns is a hindrance to law enforcement and an incentive to crime. This may be true, but it is the sort of belief for which supporting evidence is hard to find, and it is even difficult to be sure what counts as good evidence. But since emotions run high on this issue, it is a certainty that antigun organizations will continue to push legislation to make the possession of private firearms a crime. Yet other groups hardly need to lobby because, to a certain degree, they serve as arbiters concerning what is in the public interest. The American Medical Association is such a group. Even more influential is the American Bar Association. It not only serves as arbiter but, in a sense, controls the process of legislation because its members are the members of the legislatures and serve as counsels for legislative committees. Even the curbs against improper practices within the law profession are initiated by the A.B.A. And if the interests of the entire law profession are disturbed — as, say, by one who advises persons on probate and divorce matters without consulting lawyers — it is an easy matter to hang the label "unlicensed practice" on such activity and almost as easy to have it declared criminal conduct.

White Collar Crime, and Some Unhelpful Ideas About the Causes of Crime

Perhaps it is understandable that these theoretical or "philosophical" difficulties should not detain working rehabilitationists. Perhaps it is conceivable that people who haven't the slightest need for rehabilitation could commit crimes. Still, it may be claimed, and indeed is, that most criminals can be classified into definite criminal types. This can be verified by anyone familiar with the interiors of prisons. So, the rehabilitationist may contend, we grant that we don't have a theory about how to handle all offenders, but we do have ideas about how to handle most of them, especially the most serious offenders.

To dispose of this attempt to dismiss theoretical difficulties, I want now to say something about the usual criminal typologies. Almost every typology is based broadly on either a psychological theory which, perhaps a little crudely, may be summed up by saying that criminals are maladjusted or sick persons, or on a sociological theory which, also a little crudely, may be summed up by saying that criminals are the products of unfortunate environments. Some criminologists talk about the "complexity" of causes and call for the integration of psychological and sociological approaches. But whether one takes an integrated approach or adheres to either one of the two theories, one accepts the idea of criminal classes and the belief that criminals are *deviant citizens* who must unlearn unsocial patterns of behavior. No criminal typology includes a class of persons who are criminals because their activities happen to be against the law. The closest any typology comes to making allowances for this is when it recognizes the class of "occasional offenders." But occasional offenders are distinguished from "true" criminals not merely by the alleged fact that they do not ordinarily commit crimes but also, as we have seen, by the nature of their crimes. Almost every criminology text states that crime is largely a matter of definition. But this idea is conveniently ignored in the typology sections. I venture to suggest that this is because the idea of rehabilitation is unintelligible if one takes seriously the proposal that the concept of crime depends on how it is defined.

The recent trend in criminology has been to dismiss Sutherland's "white collar crime" theory. But I believe that this theory is extremely helpful in examining the idea of rehabilitation. According to Sutherland, the overwhelming majority of both serious and non-serious crimes is committed by persons outside the usual criminal classes. Among the crimes Sutherland enumerates are: illegal stock manipulations, misrepresentation in advertising, embezzlement and misapplication of funds, shortweighing and misgrading of commodities, fee-splitting in medicine,[13] restriction of competition, fraudulent reports in accident cases and indirect bribery of public officials to secure favorable contracts or legislation.

From various figures that Sutherland provides, I calculate that the total financial loss in the history of the United States from robberies, burglaries, property damage by hooliganism and protection payments to the "underworld" is not equal to the financial loss in a single year due to white collar crime, i.e., due to what Al Capone called the "legitimate rackets." Thus, for illustrative purposes, consider the fact that in 1938 public enemies one through six stole a total of $130,000. But in Chicago, during a two year period, householders lost $54,000,000 because a city official granted immunity from inspections to stores that provided his constituents with Christmas baskets. The true seriousness of this kind of crime is explained by Sutherland:

> financial loss from white-collar crime as it is, is less important than the damage to social relations. White-collar crimes violate trust and therefore create distrust, which lowers social morale and produces social disorganization on a large scale. Other crimes produce relatively little effect on social institutions or social disorganization.[14]

D. C. Gibbons says that white collar criminals do not perceive themselves as criminals and hence, he claims, they do not need resocialization.[15] Now such logic is remarkable for anyone who has faith in the idea of rehabilitation. It may indeed be true, (as I believe it to be), that white collar criminals cannot in general be rehabilitated; but if that depends solely on the fact that they do not perceive themselves to be criminals, then there is little hope for the effectiveness of rehabilitation on any widespread scale. In using the expression "the legitimate rackets," the most notorious criminal of our times made clear that he did not perceive himself to differ from others. Crimes for financial gain committed by persons in the lower economic class are not felt by them to be as disrespectable as the crimes of "robber barons." White collar crime is very influential in making lower class criminals think of themselves as victims, not offenders. "Common criminals" are keenly aware of the fact that white collar criminals are hardly ever dealt with in criminal courts. Sutherland states:

> The crimes of the upper class either result in no official action at all, or result in suits for damages in civil courts, or are handled by inspectors, and by administrative boards or commissions, with penal sanctions in the form of warnings, orders to cease and desist, occasionally the loss of a license and only in extreme cases by fines or prison sentences.[16]

It is most unreasonable to expect white collar crime to be substantially reduced through the processes of rehabilitation. White collar criminals do not come from broken homes; they do not have low intelligence and poor vocational skills; they are not psychopaths. Their crimes are the undesirable but almost natural responses to economic and competitive pressures. If such crimes are to be eliminated, it will have to be as a result of changing social organizations. But such changes are a long way off, if they are coming at all. To say, as I have actually heard some people say, that all this proves is that everyone needs rehabilitation is really to admit that rehabilitation is inappropriate as a means of dealing with crime. It would be only a figurative way of saying that society needs drastic reorganization. I agree — but this gives no support to the rehabilitation theory, understood literally. And meanwhile, rehabilitation theory gives no clues as to what actually should be done about physicians who split fees, persons who exaggerate their injuries for insurance benefits, and congressmen who take bribes.

Criminologists are fond of saying that parental neglect and exposure to criminal influence are the main factors leading to delinquent behavior. But it is plain that they use the term "criminal influence" in a biased way to refer only to those illegal activities which are much more frequent in the lower economic classes. If the white collar class were recognized as a delinquent subculture, then the notions of a delinquent subculture and exposure to criminal influence would be too broad to be useful. That is, we would have to say that growing up in America is growing up in a delinquent subculture. One commits crimes because one grows up in America. And that, I'm afraid, is a bit too rich for the blood of most criminologists.[17]

Commonly, criminologists drift off into such talk as "most crime is committed by slum dwellers" and other generalizations to that effect. This pigeon-holing stems not only from a wish to push a theory about rehabilitation but also from a desire to talk about the basic causes of crime. Without this pigeon-holing, talk of basic causes is almost absurd. Much of this talk conveniently overlooks the majority of crimes *mala prohibita*. And a criminologist knows that, if he hopes to be taken seriously, he cannot preach the end of "The American Way of Life" as the solution to the problems of crime. He may therefore concede that crime "in a certain sense of the word" is as prevalent in the government, in the judiciary, in corporations, and in the professional classes as among slum dwellers, but the scare-quotes serve to undo the force of the concession. He knows his work will be regarded as a piece of propoganda and not as a work of impartial scholarship if he claims that *most* physicians and *most* members of the judiciary need rehabilitation of one sort or another. Hence rehabilitationists concentrate on "real crime." Real crimes turn out to be what the overwhelming majority of prison inmates are serving time for. But what this proves is that, given the biased samples that prisons provide, the problems which administrators of justice impose on themselves are not coextensive with the problems in the theory of punishment.[18]

Treatment theorists are, of course, committed to something more than the view that there are basic causes of crime common to nearly all forms of criminal conduct. They also believe the causes are still operative. Thus Gibbons says that treatment "consists of tactics and procedures deliberately undertaken to change those conditions thought to be responsible for the violator's misbehavior."[19] Clearly, the "causes" such criminologists have in mind are not the events that *trigger* the criminal acts but the conditions which *sustain* the alleged criminal-mindedness.[20] Treatment workers are advised to learn "the etiological factors of *crime*." Note the interesting use of "crime" as opposed to "criminal act." When the term "crime" is substituted for "criminal act," one switches from thinking of an individual event to thinking about an ongoing problem and the conditions that sustain that problem. Once this switch is made, it is easy enough to ignore the lesson of Humpty Dumpty — that what is done cannot always be undone. Treatment workers are not advised to learn the "etiological factors of X's criminal act," and rightly so, for it is unclear what use they would make of such knowledge.

The advantage of fudging the terms "criminal act" and "crime" are, I hope, obvious. It is a device for redirecting our attention. I said earlier that the majority of the kinds of crimes as well as the majority of the number of crimes will not fit into the rehabilitationist scheme of things. The truth of this may be the more easily seen if one attends to specific events, for only then will people's highly individualistic experiences come into focus. The elusiveness of these experiences, the romantic entanglements, the unexpected financial reversements, the practical impossibility of predicting the confrontations people will have, and the highly legalistic nature of most offenses will all combine to make the notion of criminal-mindedness as the chief etiological factor in criminal behavior seem wildly implausible.

On an Alleged Philosophy of Non-Punitive Treatment

There is no one theory about rehabilitation. There is not even anything like agreement as to what rehabilitation is about. Some proponents of rehabilitation are psychiatrists who eagerly push the view that all criminal acts indicate mental illness.[21] Other proponents think that a commitment to rehabilitation is a natural corollary of a belief in determinism. Allegedly, if determinism is true, no one should ever be blamed for what he does, much less be punished. He should be reconditioned, retrained, resocialized, rehabilitated, receive treatment — whatever the favorite expression may happen to be. Yet others stress the idea that criminals have learned antisocial patterns of behavior that need to be unlearned. Accordingly, different rehabilitationists emphasize psychotherapy, group-relations therapy, religious counselling, vocational training, or just plain humane handling. And multi-causal theorists remain confident that whatever the reason for some individual's committing a criminal act, there is some uniquely appropriate treatment for his type of case.

Not all those who call themselves rehabilitationists believe that rehabilitation can completely replace punishment. They realize that it is only within a framework of involuntary detention that they can have the opportunity to rehabilitate certain offenders. They claim that we should not be concerned only with locking up a person who has committed a crime; we should put our main efforts into figuring out ways that will make him unlikely to commit a crime again. This seems to be a moderate thesis but, even so, a mistaken one. However, it is not my concern here to argue against it. Rather, I am more interested in the extreme thesis which I call the Pure Treatment Theory. This is a thesis that has had the most prominent spokesmen and certainly the most attention-getting ones. They are fond of illustrating the need for rehabilitation by citing dramatic cases of psychotic criminal behavior which they presumably mean to suggest as paradigms of criminal action. They are guilty of what Jerome Bruner has called addiction to the fallacy of the dramatic instance.[22] They seem totally oblivious of the less glamorous crimes. Yet, curiously, it is with respect to those who commit the more dramatic crimes that it is impossible to imagine getting along without prisons. Whereas it is just possible that a wealthy kleptomaniac, embarassed by his compulsion, might submit to the efforts of psychiatrists to cure him, it is hardly imaginable that a racketeer would do likewise. Of course, the racketeer may be detained against his will to undergo the "cure." But this is certainly to stretch the meaning of the non-punitive philosophy of Pure Treatment.

The term "punishment" stigmatizes those who are punished, so it is natural that treatment authorities will shun the use of the word. But, although psychiatrists decry the use of punishment *under that name,* every psychiatric hospital uses disciplinary methods well known in prisons. Hospital inmates are expected to conform to the rules and regulations of the hospital even though they may be there because psychiatrists have testified that they were not able to conform their behavior to the rules and regulations of society. Difficult patients are put into "the quiet room," (read: "solitary confinement"), or sometimes "hydrotherapy has to be administered," (read: "hosing them down").

Mental hospitals, even those for the non-criminally insane, are custodial and not treatment-oriented. Punishments are routine but, as Goffman puts it, and as the above examples make clear, they "are phrased in a language that reflects the legitimate objectives of the institution."[23] Every activity in a hospital, including a doctor's refusal to see a patient, is rationalized in terms of psychiatric theory. Again, as Goffman observes, anything may be inflicted on an inmate and made respectable by calling it treatment. In the eyes of the general public, therapy and rehabilitation are not promises held out for the future but are the *de facto* goings-on in all hospitals. Rehabilitation theorists encourage the public to view the situation in that way.[24]

Even if we ignore these punitive measures, the simple truth is that the practice of forcible detention in a total institution is punishment. That you ultimately have the individual's welfare at heart does not change things. One might as well say a mother who spanks her child is not punishing it. We cannot insist too often that the deprivation of liberty is a punishment and is not merely the opportunity to choose between imposing a punishment or administering treatment. This is not a mere verbal nicety. This way of looking at the matter provides a safeguard against the possible abuses of those who preach rehabilitation. We do need this reminder because the unfortunate fact is that the most vocal advocates of rehabilitation as replacement for punishment have preached astonishing things. Renowned psychiatrists like Karpmann and Menninger would have us create a society in which psychiatrists have the right, and even the duty, to assess the mental health of everyone. Then, if they find something called criminal-mindedness in a person, he would be removed to an appropriate institution for "preventive detention." How long is he to stay there? Until such time as he is cured? It may well amount to a life sentence. What if the potential danger is that the person is likely to be an inveterate banana stealer? It matters not, because once you see the detention in terms of quarantine and hospitalization then there is no point in talking about an injustice. Hence, while treatment perhaps is not in principle a despicable idea, its fanatic advocacy has despicable consequences.

A Typical Disagreement on a Rehabilitative Device

The aims and practices of the rehabilitationists are diverse, and there is no easy way to sum them up. Even where there is agreement about the usefulness of a certain practice, there is no agreement about the purpose of that practice and hence no way of verifying that it is useful. Consider the role of prison labor. Some penologists think its usefulness is that it provides an antidote to idleness, which is supposed to be bad for the prisoners' morale. Others defend labor as vocational training, while still others claim it develops habits of industry if not specific skills. But the fact remains that labor was originally introduced as a punitive measure and, even today, judges *sentence* men to so many years of "hard labor." What usefulness there was in the practice lay in the fact that it provided the state with a cheap labor market and easy profits.[25]

Religious counselling forms the core of the rehabilitation programs in about three hundred prisons. This, by itself, is horrible to contemplate, but the fact remains that whether the program is mainly religious counselling, or vocational training, or psychiatric therapy, or prisoner-run group relations seminars, or formal classes in good citizenship (as in many federal prisons), or improved living conditions, or half-way houses, or anything else, such programs either have been demonstrated not to work or they are of such a nature that it cannot be demonstrated whether they work or not.[26] And if it is the case that even working with the biased samples that prisons afford, rehabilitation has not been successful, isn't it reasonable to suppose that if we placed most citizens in the criminal class, rehabilitation would be yet more farfetched?

Conclusion

It is always an empirical question what sorts of acts are disruptive in and to a society. Such acts will vary with the social institutions, the physical and psychologocal make-up of the members of the society, and also with their ethical ideals and social aims. Hence what needs to be outlawed must vary accordingly. Of course, it is hard to see how murder could be insignificant in any society. But from society to society there will be variations as to what constitutes a murder. Real crime, understood as that which should be a crime *no matter how* a society is organized, is a bogus concept. It is, therefore, hard to see how it can supply the justification to the rehabilitationist's belief in criminal-mindedness.

I have been arguing against an exaggeration. Unhappily, it is a real, not a hypothetical, exaggeration. I concede that some criminals would profit from certain efforts to change them. But the thesis that rehabilitation is always needed and is always preferable to punishment is simply not coherent. Nevertheless, it is seriously advocated by "leading authorities." Finally, I worry over the morality of a rehabilitation program which is now in such a state that it is worse than punishment in ordinary prisons. And I worry, too, over the morality of men who, condemning prisons for their inhumanity, would sentence men to institutions where frequently their lives would be much worse.

NOTES

[1] T. Eriksson, "Society and the Treatment of Offenders," *Theories of Punishment* (1971), p. 266. S. Grupp, editor.
[2] *Ibid.*

³*Ibid.*, p. 267.
⁴J. Phelan, *Lifer*. Quoted in J. D. Mabbott, "Punishment," *Mind* (1939), p. 54.
⁵*Ibid.*
⁶L. McKorkle & R. Korn, "Resocialization within Walls," *Annals of the American Academy of Political and Social Science* (1954), p. 95.
⁷By a Pure Rehabilitation Theory, I refer to a theory almost no criminologist accepts; it is advocated chiefly by certain psychiatrists. According to this theory, rehabilitation *is* psychiatric treatment. Prisons are always inappropriate places for offenders. Contrarily, most criminologists regard psychiatric treatment as a part of some rehabilitation programs, and they view the rehabilitory process as something to be done mainly *within* prison walls.
⁸M. Balint, "On Punishing Offenders," *Psychoanalysis and Culture* (1951), pp. 254, 266. G. Wilbur and W. Muensterberger, editors.
⁹Because he fails to see how justice can be an issue, Karl Menninger, in "Psychiatry and the Law — A Dual View," *Iowa Law Review* 38, (1953), goes so far as to say that a person who commits even a trivial offense should be hospitalized as a patient and, if no cure is known, he may be kept there for the rest of his life. He advocated this position as far back as 1928 in "Medicolegal Proposals of the American Psychiatric Association," *Journal of Criminal Law & Criminology*. The same position is endorsed by Guttmacher and Weihofen in *Psychiatry and Law* (1952), p. 444. Perhaps fully to appreciate the difficulties in the *disease model* of criminality, we should bear in mind how precarious that model is even for the non-criminally insane. Thomas Szasz has made a career out of challenging the "myth of mental illness." See also E. Goffman's *Asylums* (1961). The most philosophically sophisticated examination of the issue is D. A. Begelman's "Meaning, Metaphors, the Medical Model, and Some Muddles," *Psychiatry* (1971).
¹⁰*Mental Health and the Offender*. Quoted in A. Flew, "Crime or Disease?" *British Journal of Sociology* (1954).
¹¹But see *infra*, note 20, for another example.
¹²One may think the "right kinds" of crimes are just those that are felonies. But just which crimes should be felonies? Anyhow, what may once be a felony may later be classified as a misdemeanor, not because of theoretical analysis but in order to relieve crowding in prisons. Furthermore, whatever the merits of the felony-misdemeanor distinction, it sheds no light on the felon-misdemeanant distinction so far as the latter is intended to explain what a "real criminal" is. We tend to suppose that misdemeanants are less in need of rehabilitation than felons. But this overlooks the fact that on one occasion a person may commit a misdemeanor and on another occasion commit a felony. The felon-misdemeanant distinction has little value, and that value is outweighed by the confusion it engenders. For more on this, see E. Sutherland and D. Cressey, *Principles of Criminology* (1955).
¹³Sutherland estimates that two-thirds of New York surgeons split fees. This violates the conditions of admittance to the medical profession and violates specific statutes in many states. It is a very serious matter because a physician will send his patients to the specialists who give him the best splits rather than to the ones who do the best work.
¹⁴E. Sutherland, "White-Collar Criminality," *American Sociological Review* (1940), reprinted in *Delinquency, Crime and Social Process* (1969), p. 353. D. Cressey and D. H. Ward, editors.

[15] *Changing the Lawbreaker* (1965), p. 270.

[16] Sutherland, *op. cit.*, p.356.

[17] The picture of America as a delinquent culture is not such an exaggeration as the reader may think. In a study of one thousand men, mostly middle-class, 91% admitted to having committed crimes, and 64% admitted to felonies. J. S. Wallerstein and C. J. Wylie, "Our Law-Abiding Law Breakers," *Probation* (1947).

[18] According to E. J. Hopkins, in *Our Lawless Police* (1931), the most significant felony engaging subculture is the police. The number of kidnapings by police is *thousands of times* greater than the number committed by other kidnapers. (I take it that an illegal arrest for the purpose of harrassment is counted as a kidnaping.) These kidnapings are a small portion of the serious crimes police commit daily. It is futile to think anything can be done about this by piecemeal arrests and/or rehabilitation of offending policemen. For that is only to acquiesce to the false cliches that "there are a few rotten apples in every barrel" and "we must weed the bad ones out." It is a refusal to face up to the full extent of these crimes, probably because it would be depressing to have to admit that rehabilitation does not go even a small way toward solving these problems.

[19] Gibbons, *op. cit.*, p. 130.

[20] Throughout his "Criminality and Mental Illness — Two Faces of the Same Coin", *Chicago Law Review* 22, (1955), Philip Roche eschews the use of the word "criminal act." He talks instead of "criminality" which seems to be, for him, some kind of undifferentiated drive to whatever is illegal. On one occasion a man may rape a small girl and at another time he may fly a kite in an area restricted to balloons. (My examples, not Roche's.)

[21] The "discovery" that criminals are all mentally ill turned out to be easy because mental health is often loosely defined as being a nice sort of chap at all times. Thus, Menninger writes, "Let us define mental health as the adjustment of human beings to the world and to each other with a maximum of effectiveness and happiness. Not just efficiency or just contentment, or the grace of obeying the rules of the game cheerfully. It is all of these things together. It is the ability to maintain an even temper, an alert intelligence, socially considerate behavior and a happy disposition. This, I think, is a healthy mind." Quoted in *Psychoanalysis, Psychiatry and the Law* (1967), p. 522, J. Katz, J. Goldstein, A. Dershowitz, editors.

[22] In *Freud and the Twentieth Century*, ed. by Benjamin Nelson (New York, 1957). For a discussion, see Donald C. Williams, "Philosophy and Psychoanalysis" in *Psychoanalysis, Scientific Method, and Philosophy*, (1959), S. Hook, editor.

[23] Goffman, *Asylums* (1961), p. 85.

[24] Some hospital administrators take a different tack and "bravely confess" that their hospitals are understaffed and/or short of facilities. Thus, they create the illusion that the only thing that keeps them from successfully treating all their patients is the unfortunate lack of material resources.

[25] In 1937, the Director of the U.S. Bureau of Prisons said that the greatest therapeutic tool of all "is just plain honest-to-goodness work," in Sutherland and Cressey, *op. cit.*, p. 522. The Director's statement exhibits the failure to face up to the fact that crime is as common among people who work regularly as among people who don't. The need-to-work theory gains what little plausibility it has from the fact that the biased prison population is made up of about 70% unskilled labor. And the theory cannot in any case explain away the other 30%. Ironically, when prisons were first

employed as the standard way of handling criminals (in about the late eighteenth century), labor was forbidden because it allegedly prevented reflection on one's sins, and such reflection was supposed to lead to repentance. Recently, penologists have argued that industrializing prisons is a barrier to treatment if for no other reason than that work interferes with time that could be spent in direct therapy. The argument rages, and it may be time to pause and ask ourselves why no system seems to be better than any other (as measured by a recidivist index).

[26] For documentation of this claim, consult the following: D. Cressey, "The Nature and Effectiveness of Correctional Techniques," *Law and Contemporary Problems* 23, (1958); D. Cressey and K. Schuessler, "Personality Characteristics of Criminals," *American Journal of Sociology* (1950); R. Cabot, "Treatment in social casework and the need of a criterion of tests of its success or failure," *Proceedings of the National Conference on Social Work* (1931); B. Coulter and E. Korpi, "Rehabilitation Programs in American Prisons and Correctional Institutions," *Journal of Criminal Law, Criminology and Police Science* (1954).

ANTONY FLEW
Delinquency and Mental Disease[1]

> "*Must the psychiatrist, then, unseat the king and actualize in the world of fact the philosopher-king of Plato's imagination . . . ? . . . if sufficiently secure in his knowledge of himself and of his field, he may dare where others dared and lost before.*"
> — *H. D. Lasswell*[2]

1. It is nowadays very common to assume, to suggest, or even to say, that all criminal activity or other deviant behavior is a symptom or expression of mental disease. I want in this present paper to consider what such claims mean; and, in particular, to press the question of what they ought to mean if the claims that a person is mentally diseased and that his behavior is produced by his mental disease are to warrant the inferences which are usually drawn therefrom. This philosophical inquiry is very relevant to practice, for many of what are diagnosed as cases of mental disease are not cases of mental disease at all; or, more modestly, they are not cases of mental disease in any sense of the expression "mental disease" which would warrant these usual inferences. In a word, my contention is this: claims that such and such is a case of mental disease presuppose the subsistence of strong analogies between this case and a typical case of physical disease; it is precisely and only in virtue of these assumed analogies that the usual conclusions are legitimately drawn; and yet the need to establish that there actually are these analogies is chronically overlooked when diagnoses of this kind are made or accepted.

2. That it is common to attribute any and every form of delinquency to mental disease is something which scarcely needs to be proved. It

will nevertheless be useful to begin with three illustrative quotations. The first comes from Dostoievsky's novel *Crime and Punishment*. It occurs in Section 6 of Part I, where Raskolnikov reflects upon his own conviction that an "eclipse of reason and loss of will-power attacked a man like some disease, developed gradually, and reached its climax a short time before the crime was actually committed; it continued the same way at the moment of the crime and for a short time afterwards, according to each individual; and then it passed off like any other disease." It is perhaps significant, in regard both to the condition of Russia in Dostoievsky's day and to the shape of things to come, that this appears to be the only suggestion in the entire book that crime is a disease of the individual rather than of society as a whole.

The second illustration comes from a source very different in kind and time and place. A few years ago a correspondent wrote to a widely syndicated American women's page advice column to complain that her husband "likes to break rules ... If there is a sign that says 'No Smoking', he lights up at once. 'Keep off the Grass' is an invitation. I have seen him step right over and stomp on the newly seeded lawn just for the devil of it ... Please tell me why he is like this, and what I can do about it." She signed herself "Married to a Nut." She got from the columnist, Mrs. Ann Landers, the characteristic reply: "The 'Nut' has emotional problems which go back many years ... He needs professional help."[3]

The third illustration is a boldly — not to say recklessly — comprehensive statement by Dr. J. R. Rees, who at various times served as Medical Director of the Tavistock Clinic in London, President of the World Federation for Mental Health, and Honorary Consulting Psychiatrist to the British Army. He said, in a set-piece lecture: "It should be stressed that all failure to comply with the rules of the game, and indeed all anti-social behaviour, whether it is noticed merely in the nursery or comes eventually to the courts of the country, is evidence of some psychological failure in the conduct of life. Crime (behavior which is prohibited by the criminal code) is the outward manifestation or sign of some disorder in the personality and character, however that may have been caused."[4]

This last is an extreme statement. No doubt it is as such atypical, and unrepresentative of the best middle of the road psychiatric opinion.[5] Yet for our purposes it is exactly what is wanted. In such an investigation of meaning it is best to begin with the strongest possible thesis. For, although some hedged and qualified version is more likely to be defensible as true, the understanding of the meaning of any such weaker contention presupposes the understanding of the meaning of its stronger associate. For example: although the guarded and cautious "It looks to me rather like a case of murder" commits the speaker to less than "It is a case of murder," the former is both semantically more sophisticated than the latter and logically parasitical upon it. You could not, that is, understand what is meant by the one unless you already understood what is meant by the other. Again, and more obviously to the present point, you could not comprehend a proposal to regard certain disfavored traits and performances as symptoms of mental disease (while assuming that in fact they are not), unless you first appreciated what would be meant and implied by saying that a trait or a performance truly and straightforwardly *is* a symptom of such a disease.

3. The first protagonist of what, for ready reference, I shall call the Rees thesis seems to have been Plato in *The Republic*.⁶ Appreciating that it was this premise which was needed in order to warrant his desired conclusions, Plato was concerned with developing and stressing the analogy between physical disease — disease of the body — and what he wanted us to admit as psychological disease — disease "of the soul." *The Republic* is officially about justice, which is taken to be the most comprehensive virtue. Half way through Book I the dialogue comes urgently alive with the intervention of the harsh debunker Thrasymachus. Apart from offering what is presumably intended as a definition of the word "justice," Thrasymachus contends that justice is not to the advantage of the just man himself, but to that of other people; that it is not a good for him, but for someone else; that it is — in the often quoted original Greek words — not an οικειον (oikeion) but an αλλοτσιον αηατθον (allotrion agathon).⁷ In a characteristic excess of cynicism, Thrasymachus seems to commit himself to maintaining that this is so not just sometimes or even generally, but always. In an equally characteristic excess, Socrates adopts the contrary position: "I do not believe that injustice is more profitable than justice, not even if one leaves it free and does not hinder it from doing what it wants."⁸

It is specifically in order to establish this contention, the contention that for the just man himself justice is always good in itself, that Plato's Socrates is in later Books set to argue that justice and injustice "are in the soul what health and disease are in the body: there is no difference."[9] For, surely, physical health is good in itself for the healthy person in the sense that, although it may also be a means to further goods, it is already good without any appeal to anything to which it may happen to be a means. Nor can this claim be refuted by referring to special circumstances in which it might turn out to be good for a person to be in some way unfit. Allow if you like —though Plato certainly would not like — that an illness which enables you to escape the draft may turn out to have been on that account good for you. Still, it would have been even better for you had you been able to avoid the draft without having had the illness.

This first point about physical disease, and hence also about psychological disease in so far as that is conceived as analogous to physical disease, is central and crucial to Plato's whole argument here. A second point is that the patient suffering from a disease, if he is to achieve any cure which would not have occurred anyway had nature been left to take her own course, or if he is to secure the artificial acceleration of any such natural improvement, does typically, though not necessarily, require the help of an expert. In as much, therefore, as psychological disease does indeed resemble physical disease, there must be room for mind (or soul) doctors as well as for body-doctors. This conclusion too is entirely Platonic in spirit.[10] But, since Plato in *The Republic* does not, I think, either distinguish any function of individual psychiatry from the general political tasks of his philosopher-kings or provide for the special training of some sub-class of psychiatrist Guardians, I here quote instead from Samuel Butler's *Erewhon*. In that imaginary land there was "a class of men trained in soul-craft, whom they call straighteners, as nearly as I can translate a word, which literally means 'one who bends back the crooked.' These men practice as medical men in England...."[11]

A third point about physical disease is the most fundamental. In some way, as we shall see, both our other two points depend on it. This third point is that disease in people necessarily involves incapacity. Consider the definitions provided in the *New English Dictionary* edited by Sir James Murray. "Health," it tells us, is "Soundness of body; that condition in which its functions are duly and efficiently discharged." "Disease" in the relevant sense is, correspondingly, "A condition of the body, or of some part or organ of the body, in which its functions are disturbed or deranged; a morbid physical condition;

a departure from the state of health, especially when caused by a structural change."

One immediate objection to this definition of "disease" is that it encompasses too much. It would include both those malfunctionings due to some congenital defect and those caused by wounds. Yet neither the man through some genetic mischance born blind nor the man suffering from a gunshot wound is as such diseased.

A second immediate objection is that such a definition fails to allow for the possibility that the actual malfunctioning may be delayed. A body may be said to be (physically) diseased either because it is now malfunctioning, or because it will malfunction if it is not suitably treated. Here, of course, death is the limiting case of malfunctioning! A doctor may sometimes know that a patient has some physical disease, maybe even a fatal disease, notwithstanding that the patient is in his own eyes now perfectly fit. It is this which provides a large part of the rationale for giving regular physical check-ups to apparently well people.

A third objection is more fundamental. Although it is surely right to pick out the idea of function as central, it is wrong to attend to actuality as opposed to potentiality.[12] The tongue of a Trappist monk is not diseased because during a penitential fast it is not employed in either tasting or talking. My cacti are not diseased because they are not soaking up water which is not there. It will be time to begin talking about disease if, when the Trappist does eventually decide to put his tongue to work, he finds he cannot, or if, when I have watered my cacti, no water is absorbed.

A fourth and far more important point about these dictionary definitions comes out when these two examples are compared. In so far as both show that what matters here is potentiality and not actuality, they are similar. But in another respect they are crucially different. Suppose that after a long drought water is supplied to my still living cacti, and that still none actually is absorbed. Then that will constitute a sufficient reason for inferring that there must be something organically wrong, although what is organically wrong will not necessarily be a disease. Contrast this with the case of the fasting Trappist. He is a person and not a plant. So the fact that he does not eat when food is provided is no more sufficient to show that there is something organically wrong with him than is the fact that he always and habitually refrains from making passes at the girls. In his case, but not in the case of the cacti, there is room for questions about what he can do if he wants and what he could do if he tried. What the comparison of these two cases shows is that an adequate account of the essential nature of physical disease in man must refer to these distinctions.

Since such distinctions, and the facts upon which they are based, are in this way essential and fundamental, it is important to point to them in the most theoretically neutral and inoffensively uncontroversial fashion of which we are capable. Even that may not be enough for those who happen to have powerful preconceptions about the putative incompatibility of freewill and determinism and about the necessity of determinism for science. Try, nevertheless, to notice that the body of anyone who is awake and not totally paralyzed is partly, although only partly, subject to the will. He can, that is to say, normally move certain parts of his body at will; although there are other parts which he can move only indirectly as a result of moving something else directly. The limbs, for instance, fall into the former category; the liver, and the vermiform appendix, into the latter.

This is one fundamental difference, universally familiar. Another equally familiar difference is that between the case in which I can truly say that I moved some part (or even the whole) of my body and the case in which I can truly claim that it moved (although I did not move it). Let us, in order to save words later, distinguish movements of the first kind as movings, while reserving the word "motions" for movements of the second sort. And let us also, while we are about it, notice the dangerous possibilities here of that favorite word "behavior" which bridges, and which may therefore lead us to neglect, this basic distinction between movings and mere motions.[13]

We are now, at last, in position to make our third point about physical disease. It is that physical disease in man typically, and perhaps essentially, involves some actual or potential incapacity. It is for this reason, surely, that physical disease is taken to be bad in itself for the diseased person himself. It is also for this same fundamental reason that, typically, he requires the services of an expert. It is because incapacities are incapacities, and because the patient who is in some way incapable cannot just snap out of his diseased condition at will, that, if there is to be a cure which would not have occurred anyway had nature been simply left to take her course, a program of treatment is required. And typically, though not necessarily, programs of treatment for the patient are prescribed and supervised by experts.

To illustrate that this third point about physical disease in man is correct, consider malingering. The malingerer is the man who reports sick although he believes that he is not. He pretends to be afflicted with some disease, or to be otherwise unfit, in order to be excused from duties which he does not wish to fulfill. His pretenses, and the response of the authorities if they are persuaded that he really is sick and not malingering, are intelligible only and precisely in so far as his pretense would involve, if it were genuine and not a pretense, some relevant incapacity.

Certainly, to be capable of doing what the diseased or otherwise unfit man cannot do always requires the structural integrity and actual or potential proper functioning of organs which never are subject to the will. Nevertheless, the criterion of the healthy man's freedom from disease is neither the structural integrity of all or any part of the organism, nor the propriety of any actual or hypothetical movements, but instead his capacities for movings or not movings. If some untoward condition of structure or behavior in a human organism or any of its organs neither directly nor indirectly gives rise to any incapacity, then that condition, however untoward, cannot be accounted a disease. So, if we are to retain any definition of "disease" in terms of the disturbance or derangement of functions, we shall have to insist that the function of whatever is normally subject to our wills is precisely to be subject to our wills; and that it is functions of this kind which are decisive in the human context.

4. However, for our purposes it fortunately is not necessary to produce a definition of "physical disease," or to provide any other full account of the concept. It is sufficient to do what I have done in Section 3, where I have spelled out three main and connected features of disease. Even if not all essential, these features certainly do all characterize the typical case. These are the three elements which together constitute the model in fact employed by most people — not only laymen but also various sorts of experts — when they come to deal with what has been diagnosed as a case of mental disease. Whatever concept of mental they may be employing in order to distinguish mental from physical disease, they are at one in assuming that if a person is diseased, whether in body or mind, then we are entitled to infer: first, that this diseased condition is bad in itself for him; second, that he needs treatment, even if it is not yet in practice possible to provide it, and third, and as some sort of foundation for the first two, that he is in respect of this condition afflicted with certain incapacities.

That this is indeed the general assumption is something else which scarcely needs to be proved; and, in view of what has been said previously, it certainly is an entirely reasonable assumption. Yet it is still perhaps worth pointing out that this —or something very much like it — was presupposed by Philippe Pinel when he ordered that his charges in the Bicêtre be unchained: "The mentally ill, far from being guilty persons who merit punishment, are sick people whose miserable state deserves all the consideration due to suffering humanity." Again, the same reasonable assumption guided the recent British Royal Commission on the Law relating to Mental Illness and Mental Deficiency when it reported, with satisfaction: "The general public now know more about mental illness and are more sympathetic to people suffering from it than ever before."[14]

More relevant to our immediate main interests is the fact that the criminal law too makes this same assumption. It is found, for instance, behind the famous McNaghten Rules, formulated by the Judges of England in 1843, and since accepted by many other Common Law jurisdictions. These provide that a man must be held criminally accountable for his actions unless he was "labouring under such a defect of reason, from disease of the mind, as not to know the nature and quality of the act he was doing, or, if he did know it, that he did not know he was doing what was wrong." These rules have been widely criticized for their exclusive attention to intellectual incapacities. So another British Royal Commission recommended that a third clause should be added: a man is not accountable for a criminal action if he was "incapable of preventing himself from committing it."[15]

The law in many if not most United States' jurisdictions appears to have been moving in the same direction and working on the same assumption. Thus in 1871 the Supreme Judicial Court of New Hampshire argued, in what was to be a very influential ruling, that: "Whether the defendant had a mental disease . . . seems as much a question of fact as whether he had a bodily disease; and whether the killing of his wife was the product of that disease was also as clearly a matter of fact as whether thirst or a quickened pulse are the product of a fever." They therefore concluded: "No argument is needed to show that to hold that a man may be punished for what is the offspring of disease would be to hold that a man may be punished for disease. Any rule which makes that possible cannot be law."[16] Judge

Bazelon, in formulating what has since been christened the Durham Rule, gave the alternative: "simply, that an accused is not criminally responsible if his unlawful act was the product of mental disease or mental defect."[17]

5. But now, although it scarcely needs to be proved that both lawyers and the public generaly assume that a diagnosis of disease, whether mental or physical, licenses the same inferences; it is not, I suspect, a matter of common knowledge that when psychiatrists inquire into the nature of mental health and disease the last thing they apparently think of is the physical paradigm.

Consider, for example, Dr. Marie Jahoda's *Current Concepts of Positive Mental Health*.[18] This is an American work, sponsored by the "Joint Commission on Mental Illness and Mental Health, as part of a national mental health survey that will culminate in a final report containing findings and recommendations for a national mental health program." The whole enterprise was five years later most authoritatively blessed when on February 5, 1963, President Kennedy issued his Message to the Congress on "Mental Health and Mental Retardation."

Dr. Jahoda begins: "There is hardly a term in current psychological thought as vague, elusive, and ambiguous as the term 'mental health'... The purpose of this review is to clarify a variety of efforts to give meaning to this vague notion." It is unfortunate, though perhaps not surprising, that she does not think to question this emphasis upon health (positive) rather than disease (negative). But it is far more unfortunate, and surely very surprising indeed, that she never once develops comparisons between mental health, as conceived in these attempts, and physical health. Neither, it seems, did any of the authorities whom she is studying. What is revealed is, as her introductory remarks suggest, a conceptual shambles. Yet she herself concludes, with a grotesque ineptness, by launching the familiar mandatory appeal for more (expensive) empirical research: "a slow and costly" striving "for more and better knowledge about the conditions conducive to mental health."[19]

What is so serious about this is that the general failure to refer to physical disease as the paradigm opens the way to understandings of "mental disease" and "mental health" in which these expressions would be definable partly or wholly in terms not of the capacities or incapacities of the patient but rather in terms of his actual behavior or of his dispositions and inclinations. Any practitioner who is in fact guided by concepts of this sort must be doing work importantly different from that of the traditional Hippocratic body-doctor. For there can be no guarantee that what such a practitioner is thereby committed to trying to cure will be a condition which is in itself and for his patient bad, and which is not directly subject to his will.

If, for instance, "mental disease" is defined in terms of maladjustment, and if adjustment is then understood as a matter of living contentedly in whatever environment surrounds you, then the supreme exemplar of mental health must have been the legendary Vicar of Bray — who progressed from promotion to promotion by the adjustment of his convictions to each successive change in the control of the Establishment. He did what student militants, and those of my colleagues who have become advocates of student power, are always urging me to do: he moved with the times!

Alternatively, the concept of mental health may be so defined as to embrace a commitment to some more particular-favored life-style, so that what counts as mental disease becomes in part a function of the ideology of the psychiatrist. The "straightening" of patients to conform with any such ideal, even when it happens to be a most admirable ideal, is a very different matter from curing victims of complaints of which they are themselves complaining. For light but nevertheless relevant relief, recall the case of 'Married to a Nut'; and ask yourself who was complaining, and who had what problem!

6. More seriously, consider some classes of cases which many psychiatrists have assigned to the category of mental disease; and which certainly could not have been so assigned had the physical paradigm been observed. One favorite move has been to categorize all sexual deviation as psychological disorder. Thus as late as 1952 the American Psychiatric Association, in its official *Diagnostic and Statistical Manual of Mental Disorder*, listed "Sexual deviation" under the general heading "Sociopathic personality disturbance" — along with antisocial reaction, alcoholism, and drug addiction.

Yet unless such expressions as "personality disturbance" are here to be construed, perversely, as simply equivalent to "nonconformity in tastes and behavior," then sexual deviation cannot be put down as any kind of psychological deficiency or psychological disease. There surely is, at least typically, no incapacity by which the deviant can be distinguished from the straight. Thus, for instance, sexual relations between men, which used to be crimes in a less enlightened period of British law, could not take place at all if the sexual apparatus of the active party were not in working order; and even the exclusive homosexual is, presumably, as able, albeit as disinclined, to engage in heterosexual intercourse as the comparably exclusive heterosexual is able, yet not willing, to undertake homosexual activity. Nor again is there any reason to believe that the expression of their respective inclinations in what — before the four-letter revolution — film advertisers used to call "acts of love" is any more, or any less, irresistably compulsive in one case than in the other. The gift of continence would seem to be equally available to both, and equally unacceptable.

We must not be misled here by our properly liberal concern that sexually deviant acts should not be punished as crimes. No doubt there would be much to be said for a psychiatrist who regularly certified as mentally sick those who would otherwise be criminally punished for such deeds. Nevertheless, the whitest of white lies is still a lie. And furthermore, although such certification carries the acceptable implication that it would be wrong to punish the "patient," it also has other implications which are both false and obnoxious. By suggesting that his various performances were in fact uncontrollable, it deprives him of part of his status and dignity as a man: it asserts that what was done, for better or for worse, was something in which he was simply the passive victim. It also suggests that his condition is bad in itself for him, without regard to any socially imposed consequences, and, consequently, that to provide straightening treatment would be to serve in the first instance not "society" but the "patient." If the fundamental claim is false, these two further suggestions lose their foundation; and all three elements are essential to the complete physical paradigm.[20]

A second class which must be excluded if we accept that paradigm is that of the psychopaths. For, as has often been pointed out (albeit to little effect), no one seems to be able to excogitate any account of psychopathy which does not implicitly or explicitly define the concept in terms of the obnoxious conduct of the psychopath. Now, in so far as this is so, an appeal to my psychopathy cannot properly serve to excuse my obnoxious conduct. Take, for example, the device regularly used in Britain in the days when suicide there was still a crime carrying severe legal consequences. By an exercise of what the lawyers privately called "pious perjury," and in order to spare the surviving relatives unfair consequences, courts would, without making any psychological investigations at all, return the verdict: "Suicide while the balance of his mind was disturbed."

The mere fact of the offense thus became, in effect, the criterion of the presence of the diseased condition which was then accepted as an excuse. Lady Wootton, in her now classical study *Social Science and Social Pathology*, speaks of the diagnosis of psychopathy as "in fact, par excellence, without shame or qualification" the model of this "circular process." It is surprising, and a fact which does much to show that the thesis of the present paper is one worth arguing, that the moral which she then draws is that "the psychopath makes nonsense of every attempt to distinguish the sick from the healthy delinquent by the presence or absence of a psychiatric syndrome, or by symptoms of mental disorder which are independent of his objectionable behavior."[21]

The true morals are quite different. If we are going to go on making this distinction, then we need to bear the physical paradigm always in mind, and, if that is our point of reference, then psychopathy just is not a mental disease. This second conclusion does not, however, prejudice the possibility of regarding psychopathy as a mental disease. It is, rather, a precondition of so doing; since you do not, for instance, broadmindedly regard a woman as married or graciously deem her to be so if she actually is. One good reason for handing psychopathic offenders over to the psychiatrists even if these offenders are not in fact mentally diseased is that, apparently: "Punishment or the threat of punishment influences their behavior only momentarily, and its more lasting effect is to intensify their vindictiveness and anti-social attitude."[22] But, if we do this for the protection of society when the offender is not mentally diseased, let no one pretend that the mind-bending reformation thereafter attempted must necessarily be either what the psychopath himself really wants or what is in that psychopath's own best interests.

A third class of doubtful candidates for inclusion in the category of mental disease is the series of manias — kleptomania, pyromania, nymphomania, satyriasis, and so on. Obviously, the crucial question here is whether the term refers only to the inclinations and to the behavior which expresses those inclinations, or whether it also refers essentially to the uncontrollable compulsiveness of that behavior or to the irresistible nature of those inclinations. It is only and precisely in so far as the latter is part of what is meant that such a mania can be accounted a mental disease and can, consequently, constitute an excusing condition. The fact that someone is so abnormal as to want something which we do not want, or that his whole relative preference structure is deviant, are sufficient to establish that he is different, but not that he is diseased. As Lady Wootton happily remarks, with reference to kleptomania, "It is by no means self-evident that the physician's yearning for valueless porcelain figures is inevitably stronger or more nearly irresistible than the poor man's hunger for a square meal or for a packet of cigarettes."[23]

7. We can now return to Rees, and to Plato before him. The entire intervening discussion must have underlined the inordinate implausibility of any extreme thesis maintaining that all delinquency, or even all crime, is a manifestation of mental disease. Unless such a contention is to be construed as an obfuscating tautology, made to measure by arbitrarily defining one of the two categorial words in terms of the other, it is certainly false. Yet the falsehood is so fundamental as to be instructive.

The first and more obvious objection is that we humans are notoriously imperfect and that we often knowingly commit many forms of delinquency. (Even if we were in this way faultless, that in itself would not guarantee that some of us would not at some times and in some places do things which were proscribed as criminal by the prevailing legal systems.) This objection did not appear formidable to Plato at this point, for he had persuaded himself elsewhere of the truth of the contrary paradox, customarily though rather misleadingly translated, "No one willingly does wrong."[24]

The second and marginally less obvious objection is that it would be a wholly unbelievable index of the prevenient beneficence of Nature if duty and interest did in fact always coincide as happily as is required by such a thesis: if, that is, to eschew delinquency were always good in itself for the individual eschewer. If this really were the truth it then would become impossible to explain how we have come to have, and so often to contrast, the concepts of duty and interest, of morality and prudence. Certainly, if all delinquency were an expression of mental disease, then a conclusion of this kind would follow. But this is a reason for reversing the argument and appealing to the falsity of the conclusion as a disproof of the premise.

Plato developed his case for this conclusion in reaction against his

Thrasymachus. Yet Plato never seized the most basic objection to the Thrasymachean claim that justice is nothing but the advantage of the stronger. It is that any attempt to define "justice" in terms of any particular individual or group interests is diametrically wrong. The point of appealing to justice is to appeal to a standard logically independent of all such particular interests and hence capable of adjudicating between them when they conflict. And wherever there is a conflict thus adjudicated, there must be at least one party for whom to do or to accept what is just must involve some sacrifice of interest.[25]

Writers in our own time would deal differently with these two objections to the Rees thesis. To the first objection they might be inclined to respond: it is not that "No one willingly does wrong," but that "No one willingly does anything." Thus Dr. Karl Menninger, one of America's most distinguished psychiatrists, in his book *The Crime of Punishment* writes: "Free will —to a lawyer ... is a given, a basic assumption in legal theory and practice. To the psychiatrist, this position is preposterous; he seeks a clear operational definition of 'free' and of 'will.'"[26]

This is no place for an extensive discussion of these matters.[27] But let us at least be quite clear here and now that any attempt at a psychological science which cannot accommodate the differences distinguished at the end of Section 3, above, thereby discredits itself. Furthermore, if it really were possible to establish their unreality then the first to be upset would be not the legal but the therapeutic professions. For, as we have seen, these differences are essential to the distinction between human health and disease, and hence to that between mental health and mental disease.

There is no similar characteristic contemporary response to the second objection; perhaps because it never occurs to the enthusiasts of orthopsychiatry to ask what the delinquent himself wants, or to distinguish what is good for society from what is good for him. Among such enthusiasts, Dr. Edward Glover was not alone in taking it as too obvious for argument that there ought to be no limits to the exercise of paternalistic power: "If we establish that prostitution is a sign of backwardness, it is incumbent on the State to use every device, psychological and sociological, to remedy the defect."[28]

Those who propose to treat as mental patients people who are not in fact mentally diseased, and those who actually are doing this, tend to argue in the opposite direction: not from, but to the patient. They believe that since they know that their own motives are impeccably Hippocratic, and since the patient is in their charge, his position must be on all fours with that of the typical patient in an ordinary (physical) hospital.[29] That missionary of orthopsychiatry, Dr. Karl Menninger, seems prepared even to state: "'I call this condition an illness just because there is a medical treatment for it, which experience has shown to be effective.'"[30]

The argument suggested, though common, is fallacious. For it is theoretically possible that my bad habits, which I could break if I wanted although in fact I do not want, could be excised by some operation on my brain. But this has no tendency to show that these habits are, in the ordinary sense both explicated and employed throughout this paper, diseases.

NOTES

[1] I have recently published a short book entitled *Crime or Disease?* (London: MacMillan, 1973). Inevitably, the present article retraverses some of the same ground, albeit in a different way. On the other hand, it is, thanks to the helpful criticism of colleagues there and at the universities of Keele and Southern California, very different from a first version given as a lecture under the Matchette Foundation at Brooklyn College. I wish to thank both that foundation and the various colleagues concerned.

[2] H. D. Lasswell, "What psychiatrists and political scientists can learn from each other," in *Psychiatry* (1938), p. 39.

[3] *The Syracuse Herald-Journal* March 27, 1963, quoted in T. Szasz *Ideology and Insanity* (New York: Doubleday Anchor, 1970), pp. 74-75.

[4] J. R. Rees, *Mental Health and the Offender* (London: Clarke Hall Fellowship, 1947), p. 6.

[5] Indeed, the author himself, having said what he did say categorically and without qualification, proceeds forthwith to deny some of the clear implications of his own assertion: "Please do not think that in my mind there is any feeling that all offenders, such as those who drive too fast in controlled areas, or those who switch on their fires during a fuel cut, need to be referred to a psychiatrist or studied by him." (Whereas in the U.S.A. brown-outs and power cuts occur in the summer and affect the air-conditioners, in England they occur in winter, and there the good citizen switches off his electric heater!). It appears that it is not philosophers only who may merit that favorite reproach of the late Professor John Austin: "First they say it. And then they take it all back!"

[6] See Anthony Kenny, "Mental Health in Plato's *Republic*," in the *Proceedings of the British Academy* (1969), pp. 229-253.

[7] Plato, *The Republic*, s 3436.

[8] *Ibid.*, s 345A.

[9] *Ibid.*, s 444C.

[10] For "to produce health is to establish the elements in the soul in the natural

relations of domination and subjection, while to cause disease is to bring it about that one rules or is ruled by another contrary to nature" (*Ibid.*, s 444D). Such ideas of manipulation by experts for our own good are both pervasive and basic in *The Republic*.

[11]Samuel Butler, *Erewhon*, Chapter X, "Current Opinions." This mischievous work was first published in 1901. It is, therefore, a remarkable example of life imitating art that in 1924 the American Orthopsychiatric Association was founded with the object of bringing together "representatives of the neuropsychiatric or medical view of crime." (Our English "ortho" comes from a Greek root meaning straight.)

[12]For further explanation of this Aristotelian distinction, see, for instance, my *An Introduction to Western Philosophy* (New York and London: Bobbs-Merrill and Thames and Hudson, 1971), pp. 100-102 and 153-155.

[13]This possibility may be even more important than the fact that to employ this word as it is thus employed by behavioral scientists is to confound into a single category both what people say and what they do — two things which in many contexts it is necessary to be ready to contrast. It often seems that these possibilities of confusion are a main source of the term's appeal; just as, surely, a main source of the appeal to behavioral scientists of the term 'drive' is that it encourages them to overlook the fact that a human desire is not an irresistible external force and hence to believe that they are nearer to developing a mental mechanics than they in fact are, or perhaps could be.

[14]*Report of the Royal Commission on the Law Relating to Mental Illness and Mental Deficiency* (London: H.M.S.O., 1957), p. 2.

[15]*Report of the Royal Commission on Capital Punishment* (London: H.M.S.O., 1953), p. 39. Notice that, although such rules are usually applicable to all criminal offenses, it is most uncommon for the defense to appeal to them in cases where the death penalty is not involved. The reason, as was recently pointed out by Abraham Goldstein of the Yale Law School, "is that the insanity defense usually brings not freedom but commitment for an entirely indeterminate period." See A.V.S. de Rueck and R. Porter eds., *The Mentally Abnormal Offender* (Boston: Little Brown, 1968), pp. 188-189.

[16]*State* v. *Jones*, 50 N. H. 369 and 394 (1871).

[17]*Durham* v. *United States*, U.S. 214 F 2d 862 (D.C. Cir. 1954).

[18]Marie Jahoda, *Current Concepts of Positive Mental Health* (New York: Basic, 1958).

[19]*Ibid.*, pp. v, 3, and 109-110.

[20]Compare Edmund Bergler's egregious essay *Homosexuality: Disease or Way of Life* (New York: Hill and Wong, 1956). Since he cannot point to either present incapacities or delayed effects — such as those which used be be thought to be the natural consequences of juvenile masturbation — in all his proposed patients, Bergler shows the paternalistic effrontery of the psychiatrist as Guardian by maintaining: "Homosexuality is not the way of life these sick people gratuitously assume it to be, but a neurotic distortion of the total personality." (P.9).

[21]Lady Wootton, *Social Science and Social Pathology*. (London: Allen and Unwin, 1959), p. 250.

[22]*Report of the Royal Commission on the Law Relating to Mental Illness and Mental Deficiency*, Minutes of Evidence, Eighth Day, p. 287.

[23]*Op. cit.*, p. 235.

[24]See for discussion of this paradox *Weakness of Will*, edited by Geoffrey Mortimore (London: MacMillan, 1971).

[25] For a fuller discussion of these Thrasymachean issues see my *Introduction to Western Philosophy*, Chapter III s 5.

[26] Karl Menninger, *The Crime of Punishment* (New York: Viking, 1968), pp. 96-97.

[27] I have recently worked over some of the fundamentals in my *Introduction to Western Philosophy*, Chapter VII; slso with special reference to crime and psychiatry in Part Three of my *Crime or Disease?*

[28] Edward Glover, *The Roots of Crime* (New York: International U.P., 1960), p. 262.

[29] See, as one illustration of this notable reluctance to recognize that there really are important and relevant differences between the status of such a typical physical patient and a person confined in an institution for the criminally insane, the exchange between Dr. Bittner and Dr. McGrath in de Rueck and Porter. *Op. cit.*, p. 128.

[30] These words are, as punctuation indicates, put into the mouth of an imaginary character in a dialogue. But there is no reason to believe that Dr. Menninger would repudiate them. *Op. cit.*, p. 136.

MICHAEL D. BAYLES
Mental Abnormality and the Criminal Process

Justice is a procedural as well as a substantive virtue. The justice of a system of criminal law does not depend solely upon who is punished and how much. It also depends upon how and by whom decisions are made as to whether or not people should be punished. Philosophers who discuss punishment frequently consider mental abnormality as an excuse. Usually their discussions center on substantive issues: Why should mental abnormality excuse a person from punishment? What types of mental abnormality should be accepted as excuses? How should the tests of exculpating mental abnormality be formulated? While these issues are undoubtedly of great importance, this paper does not focus upon them. Instead, this paper is primarily concerned with procedural matters: Who should decide whether a person is excusable due to mental abnormality? What procedures should be followed in reaching such a decision? When during the criminal process should this decision be made?

The justice of the criminal process is a form of imperfect procedural justice.[1] In imperfect procedural justice, there is an independent standard of a just result. For the present topic the general standard is that those who lack responsibility due to mental abnormality ought not be punished. The just procedures are those which are most likely to lead to just results without conflicting with other moral standards and rules. Of course, unjust procedures may lead to just results. But they are less likely to do so than just ones. So the moral problem of a just criminal process is to design procedures which are compatible with other moral values and are most likely to lead to just decisions and dispositions.

Issues concerning the mental abnormality of persons arise in various forms throughout the criminal process. To a criminal lawyer, this variety may not seem unusual; but to the uninitiated, it appears as a bewildering morass. Issues of mental abnormality may be raised at eight or more different points in the criminal process.[2] Mental abnormality may be considered by different authorities at least four times before trial. First, police exercise discretion with respect to the arrest and disposition of persons. They may not arrest a person whose conduct they believe to be the result of mental abnormality. Instead, they may refer the problem to other agencies or simply do nothing. Second, prosecutors exercise discretion concerning whether to invoke criminal or civil commitment proceedings or to refer the problem to other agencies. Third, issues of mental abnormality are sometimes raised at preliminary hearings or before grand juries. However, the issues are not as frequently raised in this way as in the first two ways. Fourth, prior to trial or at any point during it, a defendant's competence to stand trial may be considered. Usually the defendant, prosecution, or judge can raise this issue.

During trial, issues concerning a defendant's mental abnormality can be raised in two forms. First, the chief and traditional method of raising the issue is for a defendant to plead insanity as a defense. The insanity defense is always an affirmative defense, so the burden of going forward with the evidence, but not always the burden of persuasion, lies with a defendant. Different jurisdictions use different criteria or tests of insanity as an excuse. Second, some jurisdictions, e.g., California, permit raising the issue of mental abnormality in terms of diminished responsibility for some or all crimes. Unlike the insanity defense which completely exculpates from responsibility, diminished responsibility only mitigates responsibility. For example, in England diminished responsibility is only permitted for the charge of murder, and if successfully argued reduces the charge to manslaughter.

Finally, issues of mental abnormality can be raised even after conviction. A question of mental abnormality may be raised to prevent sentencing, for a person cannot be sentenced unless he is mentally competent. Mental abnormality can also be raised after sentencing, for a convicted and sentenced prisoner cannot be executed if he is mentally incompetent. Further, in some jurisdictions appeals of convictions are delayed if the appellant is not competent.

There are many problems with this complex of procedures for considering issues of mental abnormality. The several distinct issues concerning mental abnormality are often not clearly or adequately presented; as a result they may be confused with one another. One issue concerns a person's present competency. This issue is involved in determining whether or not a person is capable of standing trial, being sentenced, being executed, or making an appeal. The tests of competency are roughly the same in almost all jurisdictions. These tests are whether the defendant can understand the nature and object of the proceedings against him and is able to participate rationally in his defense.[3]

A second issue concerns a person's possible lack of responsibility due to mental abnormality when he committed an act. This issue is involved in the insanity and diminished responsibility defenses. Different jurisdictions, however, use different tests of such responsibility. The M'Naghten test is the oldest and most widely used. The M'Naghten rules declare that a person lacked responsibility for an act if he "was labouring under such a defect of reason, from disease of the mind, as not to know the nature and quality of the act he was doing, or if he did know it, that he did not know he was doing what was wrong."[4] Contrary to the opinion of the original court, "wrong" is usually interpreted to mean legally wrong. In addition to the M'Naghten test, some jurisdictions use the so-called "irresistible-impulse" test. Even if a person knew the nature and quality of his act and knew that it was wrong, the irresistible-impulse test excuses him if as a result of mental disease he did not have the power or capacity to choose or control his behavior.[5]

There are two other tests of lack of responsibility due to insanity. The Durham test maintains that a person is not criminally responsible if his act was the product of a mental disease or defect.[6] This test has not been widely adopted and was recently overruled.[7] It obviously changes the form of the question of responsibility to what is and is not a mental disease or defect. The final test is that proposed in the Model Penal Code. Essentially combining the M'Naghten and irresistible-impulse tests, it is becoming more widely accepted as penal codes are revised. This test declares that a person is not criminally responsible for conduct if as a result of mental disease or defect he lacked substantial capacity to appreciate the criminality of his conduct or to conform his conduct to the law.[8]

Besides these insanity defenses, diminished responsibility also concerns the same general question. For the most part diminished responsibility has been restricted to homicide cases. However, the Model Penal Code would permit evidence of mental disease or defect whenever it is relevant to a defendant having had a state of mind which is an element of the offense, e.g., intent.[9] Such an extention of diminished responsibility might allow complete exculpation in some cases; for the lowest class of crimes cannot be reduced, and, therefore, the only permissible disposition would seem to be complete exculpation.[10]

A third issue of mental abnormality concerns the grounds for involuntary commitment to a mental institution. This issue is not strictly one of criminal law, but it is directly relevant. The grounds for such commitment are very diverse and imprecise. They vary from dangerousness to simply being mentally ill.[11] But whatever the grounds for civil commitment, in fact, when someone is judged to be mentally abnormal by any test and at any point in the criminal process, he is usually committed to a mental institution.

These three issues of mental abnormality are distinct and should be kept separate. First, competency to stand trial or be sentenced clearly concerns a person's present mental abnormality. A person may presently be mentally ill but may not have been so when he committed a criminal act. Likewise, he may have been mentally ill and not responsible when he committed an act but may presently be normal. Yet these two distinct issues are rarely separated when psychiatrists make pretrial examinations. Second, it is also obvious that whether or not a person was insane when he committed a criminal act is not the same issue as whether he should be institutionalized. If he were insane when he committed an act but presently normal, there is no reason for his being committed. Yet, almost anyone who successfully pleads insanity as a defense will be committed to a mental institution for an indefinite period of time. Finally, the issue of present competency is not necessarily the same as that of need for commitment. A person may be incapable of understanding or assisting in a trial but not need to be institutionalized. He may be harmless and only require out-patient treatment. Indeed, commitment may retard a person's recovery since total institutionalization is not always the best method of treatment.

There are other problems and objections to the current procedures in the criminal process for considering mental abnormality. The alternatives of decisions of incompetency to stand trial and civil commitment present strong temptations to a prosecuting attorney. Decisions of incompetency or civil commitment are easier to obtain than criminal convictions. Thus, a prosecutor may seek to have a person declared incompetent to stand trial or civilly committed rather than risk a weak case in court.[12]

The insanity defense presents several problems and defects. If a defendant were mentally ill when he committed the act for which he is being tried, then even though he may be competent to stand trial he may not be very stable. The trauma of a trial may be enough to push him "over the edge." The trial of the insanity defense frequently turns into a "battle of experts." Both prosecution and defense parade psychiatrists before the jury to testify that the defendant was or was not responsible at the time of his action. Frequently, the psychiatric testimony is beyond the comprehension of the jury. Further, psychiatrists are sometimes asked to judge the responsibility of a defendant at the time of his act. But questions of responsibility are not within the province of psychiatry. Questions of responsibility are legal-moral ones. Hence, legal-moral issues become confused with psychiatric theories.[13] Finally, as previously noted, defendants are understandably reluctant to plead insanity, since, if successful, they are likely to be incarcerated for a longer period than if found guilty of the criminal charge. Hence, many who are, in fact, entitled to the insanity defense fail to raise it.

Due to these problems, among others, in recent years various lawyers, psychiatrists and philosophers have been led to advocate abolishing the insanity defense. Some commentators have gone so far as to recommend abolishing the requirement of *mens rea* and all its associated defenses, i.e., the requirement that a person act purposefully, knowingly, recklessly, or negligently.[14] H. L. A. Hart has presented generally sound objections to this proposal.[15] Hence, it will not be considered here. Others, including Hart, have advocated the weaker thesis that the insanity and diminished responsibility defenses be eliminated.[16] Under this weaker proposal, as well as the stronger one, mental abnormality would be considered for sentencing but not for conviction.

Various objections have been raised to Hart's weaker proposal to eliminate only the insanity and diminished responsibility defenses. First, such a procedure would tend to blur the distinction between those who are responsible for their undesirable behavior and those who are not. Both those who were responsible and those who were not due to mental abnormality would be convicted. Second, as Hart notes about the stronger view, mentally abnormal persons would suffer the social hostility usually expressed towards criminals.[17] Third, mentally abnormal persons would still suffer the traumata of a criminal trial and being judged guilty of a crime.

Fourth, a defendant's mental abnormality may well be relevant to conviction, for if he were mentally ill he may not have had the requisite *mens rea*.[18] That is, a mentally abnormal person may not have known what he was doing and so not have acted intentionally. Hart might avoid this objection by stipulating that only mental abnormalities which do not involve cognitive disability be excluded from the conviction process. But this alternative would still let loose dangerous persons suffering from cognitive impairment unless detainment for medical treatment were mandatory or unless persons who successfully raised such a defense were at least screened before being released. Further, any distinction between cognitive and emotional impairment would meet with strong resistance from those psychiatrists who view mental capacities as integrated. Finally, in the United States elimination of *mens rea* or the insanity defense would probably be deemed unconstitutional as denying due process.[19]

From the foregoing discussion certain desiderata for criminal procedures concerning mental abnormality may be derived. (1) The distinction between those who were and were not responsible for proscribed acts should be kept clear.[20] (2) The needs of social defense should not be ignored. That is, the public should be protected from those who are both mentally abnormal and dangerous. (3) The trauma of a criminal trial as well as the social hostility and ignominy consequent upon conviction should be avoided for those who are mentally abnormal. (4) Although the issue of mental abnormality as an excuse is one of responsibility and therefore a legal, not a medical, question, it is desirable to avoid confronting juries with complex psychiatric issues and the "battle of experts." (5) The rights of the mentally abnormal to a fair hearing and other procedural safeguards should be protected. (6) Finally, the issues of present competency, past lack of responsibility, and need for commitment should be kept distinct.

The current trend in criminal procedure is to remove more and more mentally abnormal persons from the criminal process prior to trial. This removal is being accomplished by placing greater reliance upon civil commitment and determination of incompetency. The President's Commission on Law Enforcement and the Administration of Justice has recommended strengthening this trend. Specifically, the Commission stated:

> ... if an individual is to be given special therapeutic treatment, he should be diverted as soon as possible from the criminal process. It believes further that screening procedures capable of identifying mentally disordered or deficient offenders as early in the process as possible can be improved by training law enforcement and court officers to be more sensitive to signs of mental abnormality and by making specialized diagnostic referral services more readily available to the police and the courts.[21]

However, it is unrealistic to expect police, prosecutors, and judges to have such training that they can competently make decisions about the mental abnormality of offenders. In practice, psychiatric recommendations are often adopted without question. Further, the present practice of single psychiatric examinations tends to confuse the issues of competency to stand trial and responsibility for actions.[22] Finally, the rights of those judged mentally abnormal are not protected.

Nonetheless, deciding issues of mental abnormality early in the criminal process is the only method which will meet all the desiderata for an acceptable or just procedure. Once the determination of issues is postponed to the trial stage or later, it is impossible to meet the desiderata of avoiding the trauma of a trial, the "battle of experts," etc. Thus, the suggestion here is that the insanity and diminished responsibility defenses be eliminated and a pretrial mental abnormality hearing be instituted. This hearing would be before a panel composed of psychiatrists, lawyers, and laymen. Membership on the panel would be for a definite period of time such as three years. One lawyer, layman, and psychiatrist could be changed each year. The chairman of the panel should always be a lawyer (preferably a judge) in order to ensure that proper leagal procedures are followed. Psychiatrists are included in the panel so that some members will have an excellent understanding of medical testimony. Laymen are included because the question of lack of responsibility is a legal-moral one, and the public has interests to be protected.

The panel would be empowered to determine all three issues of mental abnormality — present competency, responsibility, and commitment. But the issues would be kept distinct by requiring that each issue be determined separately and a brief, written opinion be provided. Thus, the panel would combine the functions of judge and jury with respect to questions of mental abnormality. Further, the panel would be empowered to make a proper disposition in accordance with its finding on each issue. A finding that the defendant is normal in all respects would result in his being subsequently tried on the facts. If a person is found to have been mentally abnormal and not responsible at the time of his act but presently normal, the panel would be empowered to release him.[23] If he is found to be presently abnormal, then the question of disposition would still have to be settled separately. The panel would be empowered to order commitment to a mental institution if the person is dangerous, an appropriate form of out-patient therapy, or complete release.[24] Finally, it is recommended that if a person were responsible at the time of his act but is presently abnormal, he not be prosecuted when and if he is cured.[25]

Just procedures should ensure that, as well as can be determined, all who are mentally abnormal be eliminated from the criminal process. Thus, the defense, prosecution, or judge at a preliminary hearing would be entitled to request a hearing on the issue of present incompetency. Only the defense would be entitled to request a hearing on the issue of lack of responsibility at the time of the alleged act. And if the defense did not raise that issue, the panel would not consider it. All requests for a hearing would be automatically granted. There would be a mandatory, impartial psychiatric examination of the accused only if an issue of mental abnormality were raised — not, as is currently the practice in some jurisdictions, for all persons accused of certain crimes. However, the accused would retain the rights against self-incrimination, e.g., the right to refuse to cooperate in the examination, and to be examined by his own psychiatrist as well. Further the defendant would have the right to have counsel present during all examinations. Finally, the rules of evidence before the panel would be much broader in scope than those for criminal trials. They would be more like the rules of evidence now used for presentencing.

There are numerous advantages to this proposed procedure for handling the issues of mental abnormality. First, it centralizes the procedures for handling the issues to a specific point in the criminal process. Thus, it avoids the ambiguity, uncertainty, and waste of time which are characteristic of current practice. Second, issues of mental abnormality are decided by a group of persons as well qualified as possible to decide them. Currently these issues are decided by judges or juries. The problems of jury decisions have already been noted. There is no reason to believe that judges are the best qualified to make these decisions.[26] Judges are most competent to determine whether or not proper procedures have been followed and a defendant's rights protected.

Finally, the proposed procedure meets all the previous desiderata for an acceptable or just procedure. The distinction between those who are responsible and those who are not is preserved, for only the responsible would go to trial. The needs of social defense are met since the panel can order commitment. But commitment is confined to clear cases of social defense, i.e., persons who are dangerous to others or themselves. The trauma and consequent social hostility and ignominy of a criminal trial or conviction are avoided for those who are mentally abnormal. Juries are not subject to the "battle of experts," yet there is full psychiatric input to the decision process. Mentally abnormal persons receive due process and have their other rights protected. And finally, the questions of present competency, past responsibility, and need for commitment are kept distinct.

However, there are a number of possible objections to the proposed procedure. None of them appear to present an insurmountable obstacle, but their consideration will help elucidate the proposal and show how it might be modified or expanded, if need be, to avoid difficulties. It may be objected that the procedure would still expose persons charged with crimes to too great a chance of civil commitment. In particular, permitting the prosecutor to raise the issue of competency to stand trial provides him with too much discretion. Also, prosecutors would have great opportunity to "blackmail" defendants into guilty pleas. And finally persons charged with lesser crimes would thus be subject to indefinite confinement if the prosecutor decided to ask for such a hearing.

For a number of reasons this does not seem persuasive. (1) Under current law in most jurisdictions prosecutors can raise the issue of present competency to stand trial, so the proposed procedure does not give them any more power than they now have. (2) Prosecutors are not given the power to raise the issue of lack of responsibility at the time of an alleged act. The power to raise that issue rests solely with the defendant. In the United States, it would probably be unconstitutional to permit anyone but the defense to raise that issue.[27] (3) Since the issues of present competency and need for commitment are kept distinct, a finding of incompetency to stand trial will not automatically result in commitment. Further, the proposed test for commitment is that a person constitute a danger to others or himself. By a danger to himself is meant a physical danger. If a person cannot manage his financial affairs, he need not be committed. The panel can appoint a guardian of his financial interests. (4) In current practice decisions concerning competency and commitment are often made by a judge upon recommendation of the examining psychiatrists.[28] Having a panel decide the issue and present a brief, written opinion would make it less likely the psychiatric recommendation would be followed without question.

One could modify the proposal by simply not permitting a prosecutor to raise the competency issue, but there are arguments against that modification which should not be overlooked. First, a person who is incompetent is, by definition, not capable of making a reasonable decision on that point. Second, some people may be mentally abnormal but fear the possibility of an indefinite commitment. Part of that fear could and should be allayed by reform of mental institutions. But this reform should take place independent of any change in the criminal process. This fear could be further allayed by empowering the panel only to order commitment for a definite period, say, three years, and requiring it to review all cases of persons who have not been cured in that length of time. Third, considerations of social defense and humanitarianism support the prosecutor's right to raise the competency issue. If persons are mentally abnormal and dangerous to others, they should be confined. Further, if they are mentally abnormal but not dangerous, they should be provided any available treatment. An the panel would have alternative forms of treatment available.

A second objection pertains to the possible operation of the system. The persons appointed to the panel are apt to be less competent psychiatrists and lawyers. For example, most of the court psychiatrists in Ohio are not even certified by the state. Also, the panel is apt to commit rather than take a chance on having released persons harm others.

On the contrary, the proposed procedure avoids these problems better than the current practice. First, the psychiatrists and lawyers on the panel are not to be full-time state employees as the examining psychiatrists are. Hence, the psychiatrists on the panel may be more competent than the examining ones, and the examining psychiatrists' opinions would be subject to more careful and expert scrutiny than is currently the practice where their recommendations are often automatically accepted. Second, even now there is a stong tendency to commit rather than take a chance on further harm. That will always be the case in any commitment procedure. But if the criterion for commitment is narrowed to dangerous to others or self and a written opinion is required, it will be more difficult to commit rather than take a chance.

A third objection pertains to cases involving mixed defenses, i.e., when a defendant wishes to raise other defenses in addition to insanity. If a defendant wishes to raise the insanity issue, under the proposed procedure he would apparently have incriminated himself were the panel to decide he was responsible. However, this problem is not as great as might be thought. It is becoming common practice to require the defense to inform the prosecution in advance that it intends to raise the insanity issue. Thus, a defendant must usually decide early whether or not he will raise the insanity defense. Further, in most cases in which the insanity defense is raised, it is the sole or main defense. So a person who wished to raise the insanity defense and was found responsible by the panel would probably plead guilty. Procedures also could be instituted to ensure that the pretrial mental abnormality hearing did not preclude the possibility of other defenses at trial. The easiest method would be to exclude from the trial all evidence acquired by the psychiatric examination. The prosecution would then have to proceed on evidence collected independently of the psychiatric examination. This procedure would afford the defendant as much protection from information brought out by the psychiatric examination as is currently afforded for coerced confessions.

The fourth objection is that the proposed procedure eliminates the possibility of the defense of diminished responsibility. But, it may be said, diminished responsibility really goes to the core of the requirement of *mens rea*. There are at least three lines of reply to this objection. First, and least plausibly, it may be wise in any case to eliminate or not to allow the diminished responsibility defense. Its operation appears to involve all sorts of difficulties. It is, after all, a move towards subjective liability, and it may well be that subjective liability simply cannot be considered in the criminal process. Further, diminished responsibility rests upon the distinction between general and specific intent, and that distinction is neither clear nor free from attack.[29]

Second, one could allow the diminished responsibility defense but not permit any expert testimony. The panel would have screened the defendant for severe forms of mental abnormality, and those which would be appropriate to diminished responsibility may not require expert testimony. Third, and this method seems preferable, one could allow the panel to make a binding recommendation to the prosecution as to a defendant's diminished responsibility. Since diminished responsibility operates to negate a specific mental element in a crime and so reduce the charge, the prosecution could be required to proceed only on a lesser charge as approved by the panel. Thus, the question of the presence or absence of the disputed mental state would never enter into the trial.

The fifth and final objection to be considered is that the proposed procedure is unjust or unconstitutional. Specifically, the procedure involves a denial of due process by prohibiting a trial of the insanity issue by a jury of one's peers. Indeed, in the *Lange* decision a Louisiana statute similar to the current proposal was found unconstitutional on such grounds.[30] However, it is not clear that the current proposal would be unconstitutional. And if it were unconstitutional, it could be modified to avoid the objections without seriously impairing its general operation.

There are significant differences between this proposal and the Louisiana statue which may avoid the constitutional problems. The Louisiana statute empowered a panel composed of the superintendents of state mental institutions or any competent physicians they named in their place to decide the issues of mental abnormality. If the panel found that a person was presently sane and sane at the time of his act, the decision was binding upon courts. This binding decision was found to violate the Louisiana Constitution, not the U. S. Constitution. Specifically, the court found that the statute violated the jurisdiction of state courts and the right to a trial by jury. Since the courts were given jurisdiction over criminal matters, a binding decision by the panel violated the courts' jurisdiction.[31] Further, the Louisiana Constitution provided for jury trials in some criminal cases, and, it was held, where an offense is triable by jury all defenses such as insanity must also be tried by jury.[32]

The current proposal avoids the first ground for the Louisiana decision since the panel can be constituted as a court. That is, the panel itself would constitute a special court so there would not be a decision by an independent panel binding upon a court. Further, this ground upon which the *Lange* decision rests may involve a matter peculiar to the Louisiana Constitution. The second ground of the *Lange* decision presents a more formidable problem. However, the U. S. Supreme Court has shown considerable tolerance for various methods of handling mentally abnormal persons. And there are a couple of arguments for the constitutionality of the proposed procedure which the Supreme Court might accept. Since the panel does not have the power to convict in a criminal offense, it is not a criminal proceeding and does not involve a denial of the right to a trial by jury in criminal proceedings. Also, a panel determination of mental abnormality does not preclude a trial by jury on the substantive criminal question. At most, one specific defense is removed. Presentation of the insanity defense before a jury would have to be shown to be a requirement of substantive due process before the proposed procedure could be declared unconstitutional.

Even if the above arguments were found insufficient, the functioning of the panel would not be much affected. The proposal need only be changed to permit defendants to raise the insanity defense at trial.[33] It is highly unlikely that many defendants would do so after an adverse decision by the panel, for the panel's decision and evidence could be admitted as evidence for the prosecution if a defendant raised the insanity defense. Thus, the defendant would have to present a strong case to outweigh the panel's decision allowing this possibility might even be beneficial as a form of appeal from the panel's decision. The panel would then be encouraged to decide doubtful cases in favor of defendants. The chief danger would be that the panel might tend to commit or release persons rather than find them sane and competent to stand trial. That danger does not appear to be great, but, in any event, it cannot be accurately determined before gaining actual experience with the operation of the proposal.

In summary, current procedures for handling issues of mental abnormality are not adequate to the tasks of protecting defendants' rights and eliminating mentally abnormal persons from the criminal process. A pretrial mental abnormality hearing would, by centralizing the proceedings and instituting more humane treatment of mentally abnormal persons, make the criminal process more just.

NOTES

An earlier version of this paper was read to the Third Annual Colloquium in Philosophy, University of Dayton, October, 1972.

[1] John Rawls, *A Theory of Justice* (Cambridge, Mass.: Belknap Press of Harvard University Press, 1971), pp. 85-86.

[2] For more detailed accounts of the various points at which mental abnormality may be considered see Abraham S. Goldstein, *The Insanity Defense* (New Haven: Yale University Press, 1967), ch. 11; and Samuel J. Brakel and Ronald S. Rock, eds., *The Mentally Disabled and the Law*, revised edn. (Chicago: University of Chicago Press, 1971), ch. 11.

[3] Brakel and Rock, *Mentally Disabled*, pp. 408-09.

[4] *M'Naghten's Case*, 10 Clark and Fin. 200, 209 (1843), in *Freedom and Responsibility*, ed. Herbert Morris (Stanford, Cal.: Stanford University Press, 1961), p. 395.

[5] *Parsons* v. *State*, 2 So. 854, 866-67 (Ala. 1887); *Davis* v. *United States*, 165 U. S. 373,378 (1897).

[6] *Durham* v. *United States*, 214 F. 2nd 862, 874-75 (D. C. Cir. 1954).

[7] *United States* v. *Brawner*, 471 F. 2nd 969 (D. C. Cir. 1972) Substituted the model Penal Code tests.

[8] American Law Institute, *Model Penal Code*, Proposed Official Draft (Philadelphia: American Law Institute, 1962), Section 4.01.

[9] *Ibid.*, Section 4.02 (I).

[10] Goldstein, *Insanity Defense*, p. 201.

[11] Nicholas N. Kittrie, *The Right To Be Different* (Baltimore: Johns Hopkins Press, 1971), pp. 66-68.

[12] For a discussion and illustration of possible abuses by prosecutors of the incompetency procedure to avoid a trial see Thomas S. Szasz, *Law, Liberty and Psychiatry* (New York: Collier Books, 1963), ch. 13.

[13] This comment is not intended to imply that psychiatric theories do not sometimes rest upon moral assumptions, e.g., as to what constitutes abnormal behavior. Sometimes they do, and then psychiatric testimony is simply a disguised attempt to pursuade the jury to accept the psychiatrist's viewpoint for a particular case. The crucial point is that psychiatrists *per se* are no more qualified, and perhaps less qualified, than judges and jurors to decide questions of responsibility within the legal-moral framework of the criminal law. Misunderstandings about the competence of psychiatrists are fostered by a confusion about the term "insanity" and its cognates. "Insanity" is not a medical but a legal term ascribing lack of responsibility according to one or more of the legal tests. However, many laymen and some lawyers think that it is a medical term and, therefore, that psychiatrists have special competence to determine questions of insanity.

[14] For example, Barbra Wootton, *Crime and the Criminal Law* (London: Stevens and Sons, 1963), and Karl Menninger, *The Crime of Punishment* (New York: Viking, 1968).

[15] H. L. A. Hart, *Punishment and Responsibility* (Oxford: Clarendon Press, 1968), pp. 181-185, 200-09.

[16] Hart, *Punishment and Responsibility*, esp. p. 205; Szasz, *Law, Liberty and Psychiatry*, ch. 10.

[17] Richard A Wasserstrom, "H. L. A. Hart and the Doctrines of Mens Rea and Criminal Responsibility," *University of Chicago Law Review* 35 (1967-68): 124.

[18] Joel Feinberg, *Doing and Deserving* (Princeton: Princeton University Press, 1970), p. 268.

[19] *State* v. *Strasburg*, 110 Pac. 1020 (Wash. 1910); *Sinclair* v. *State*, 132 So. 581 (Miss. 1931).

[20] "Eliminating the insanity defense would remove from the criminal law and the public conscience the vitally important distinction between illness and evil...." Goldstein, *Insanity Defense*, p. 223.

[21] *The Challenge of Crime in a Free Society* (New York: Avon Books, 1968), p. 332.

[22] Brakel and Rock, *Mentally Disabled*, p. 410.

[23] Any test of responsibility — M'Naghten, irresistable-impulse, Durham, or Model Penal Code — could be used. However, a test similar to that of the Model Penal Code seems preferable. That test is closely related to the traditional moral excuses based on the principle that responsibility implies ability, for a person incapable of appreciating the criminality of his conduct or controlling his behavior cannot comply with the law.

[24] The test for civil commitment need not be restricted to dangerousness, but that test seems preferable. It would greatly reduce prosecutors' ability to obtain commitments rather than risk weak cases at trial. See Kittrie, *Right To Be Different*, p. 402.

[25] *Ibid.*, p. 403.

[26] *Ibid.*, p. 82.

[27] *Lynch* v. *Overholser*, 369 U. S. 705 (1962). See Goldstein, *Insanity Defense*, pp. 186-88.

[28] Nine jurisdictions currently use a panel to decide competency to stand trial. Brakel and Rock, *Mentally Disabled*, p. 414.

[29] Jerome Hall, *General Principles of Criminal Law*, second edn. (Indianapolis: Bobbs-Merrill, 1960), pp. 142-44.

[30] *State* v. *Lange*, 123 So. 639 (La. 1929).

[31] *Ibid.*, p. 641.

[32] *Ibid.*, p. 642.

[33] There is precedent for this method, *State* v. *Toon*, 135 So. 7 (La. 1931).

T. L. S. SPRIGGE
Punishment and Moral Responsibility

The Principle of Responsibility

"A man ought not to be punished for doing or causing something unless he was morally responsible for doing or causing it. The less he was morally responsible for doing or causing something, the less severely can it be justifiable to punish him." For convenience, let us call this the principle of moral responsibility.

It would seem that to say, in the sense which is relevant here, that a man was morally responsible for doing or causing something is to say that his activity therein can properly be brought under various moral predicates, as being morally creditable to him, or as being reprehensible. In practice, and arguably in principle, the question tends only to arise where the action is *prima facie* a bad one, and the question is whether he was to blame or not. To be to blame is to be morally answerable in some sense for evil brought about, but it is doubtful if one can be spoken of as answerable for good brought about.

Presumably one is to blame for something if one is rightly blamed for it, so it is important to know what we mean by "blaming." As a rough working definition, intended to be as neutral as possible between various rival views, I suggest that one blames someone, it may be oneself, for doing or causing something, if one feels angry, resentful, or reproachful with him for doing or causing it and holds that one's emotional response is appropriate. One feels, moreover, that the one blamed ought to be ashamed of himself and should seek to make reparation if possible. The blame is expressed if these emotions and opinions are put into words or otherwise conveyed to others.

It may be well now briefly to offer a definition of "punishment." It might seem, at first blush, that one may describe someone as being punished for doing or causing something provided only that he did do it or cause it (one might add: or is believed to have done so by those described as imposing the punishment, though certainly the punishment will be wrongful if the belief is false); that doing or causing it was against the law of his society, or against the explicit or implicit command of some authority to which he is subject; and that on account of his having done or caused it, some form of suffering or deprivation (described as the punishment) is imposed upon him by a person or persons designated by the law or the authority (it could be by the authority itself) to impose such suffering or deprivation upon those who so act or upon him in particular. Upon the whole, however, it seems necessary to add that such suffering or deprivation is not punishment unless those who impose it, and all those who are prepared to call it a rightful punishment, deem it some kind of disgrace to undergo it.

Complete conformity to the principle of moral responsibility is not even supposed to be a feature of English Law,[1] though some may think that it ought to be, yet many aspects of the theory and practice of the criminal law would seem to rest upon it. One would expect, in any case, that most people would agree that it is *prima facie* undesirable for criminal responsibility or liability, i.e., liability to the sanctions of the criminal law, to exist in the absence of moral responsibility, even if there are special cases where this may have to be endured for good reason. In this paper I shall consider this principle of moral responsibility in regard to its association with various rival views of punishment and related matters. The principle, or some version of it, can certainly be supported in the context of very different theories. Some have even offered it as a ground for not punishing at all, asserting that the moral responsibility necessary for punishment is a myth.

Contra-indications of Moral Responsibility

The practical result of various interpretations of the principle of responsibility is more easily stated negatively than positively. When a man has done or caused something for which we are inclined to blame him, there are a variety of grounds on which we may come to believe that he was not to blame (or not so much to blame) after all. According to the principle of responsibility, such grounds would make it improper to punish a man, (or to punish him so severely) for doing or causing something which would otherwise be punishable. Let us now attempt to list the main broad headings under which the grounds of such claims for blamelessness (absolute or comparative) fall, with some additional indication, by way of example, of ways in which these are or are not reflected in actual procedures for disposing of offenders in Britain. Although each of these is considered a contraindication of blameworthiness by some, they are by no means generally accepted as such.

1) One did not know (and could not reasonably have been expected to know) that one was doing or causing the something in question.

Various features of English law reflect, or could be supported by reference to, this consideration, or even to a stronger version of it without the parenthetical clause. First is the fact that offenses against the law do not normally consist merely in certain movements (or failures to move) together with certain consequences thereof, but in actions, that is, in movements having certain results and expressing certain intentions. Thus in many cases an offense is only committed where there was an intention to act either in the prohibited way or in a prohibited way closely related thereto (e.g., there cannot be murder without an intention to cause, at the least, grievous bodily harm). There is also a general principle of problematic scope according to which there is no offense without *mens rea*, which means roughly that there was no intention to act in a prohibited way. The M'Naghten rules allow for a verdict of "not guilty by reason of insanity" when "the accused was labouring under such a defect of reason, from disease of the mind, as not to know the nature and quality of his act," though in fact this is now among the least usual ways of dealing with those deemed insane.

2) One did not know (and could not reasonably have been expected to know) that doing or causing the something in question constitutes an offense.

English law only allows for this case as such when the ignorance is due to disease of the mind and concerns the illegality of the act. Moralists doubtless disagree on this kind of issue, but many would hold that a man is not to blame for an offense which he could not be expected to recognize as morally wrong, and, even then, should not be punished for it unless he could reasonably be expected to recognize it as illegal or forbidden by the relevant authority.

3) One's action was performed in special circumstances which make it less reprehensible or not reprehensible at all. For example:

a) one acted under constraint or duress, that is, when subjected to extreme threats from someone in a position to carry them out;

b) One acted in self-defense;

c) One acted aggressively under extreme provocation.

Such considerations receive recognition in English law either through offenses being defined so as to exclude such cases, or through the existence of special forms of defense, or through a ruling that mitigating circumstances apply when the court decides upon the type and amount of punishment.

4) One could not help doing or causing what one did or caused, or at least one had a reduced ability to help it. The kind of cases sometimes brought under this head are rather various. Each of the following would be put forward in this connection by some:

a) "Actions" which are not properly actions because done in a state of automatism. In English law there is a defense of automatism which may arise when an "action" was done in sleep, an epileptic fit, etc.

b) Actions done under irresistible momentary impulse. In Britain the law makes no explicit allowance for this, but in some legal systems it is a recognized form of defense. However, some cases which a moralist might thus describe are perhaps specially treated even in Britain, when it comes to sentencing, under such descriptions as provocation, mental disorder, etc.

c) Actions stemming from mental disorder.

The question of how certain mental disorders are to be distinguished from moral failure, or if they are to be so distinguished (and if not, whether it is the concept of such mental disorder or of such moral failure which is to be discarded) is among the most vexing in this area. If all moral failure becomes illness, it is fair to say that the concept of moral responsibility is at an end, since illness is virtually by definition an object of sympathy, not of blame.

(We may note in passing, and without pursuing the matter further, that in the famous *Durham* case, in 1954, the U.S. Court of Appeal for the District of Columbia ruled quite simply that "an accused is not criminally responsible if his unlawful act was the product of mental disease or defect."[2]) In Britain the belief that an offense springs from mental disorder may have such consequences as the following:[3]

(a) The police may drop prosecution of the supposed offender. His offense may, nonetheless, reveal medical evidence which leads to his compulsory detention in a mental hospital.

(b) A convicted offender may be the subject of a hospital order or a restriction order if there is appropriate medical evidence that he suffers from a mental disorder falling within one of several recognized categories.

(c) An offender may be put on probation on the condition that he receive psychiatric treatment.

(d) There are various special defenses relative to mental abnormality. One may be found "not guilty by reason of insanity" according to the M'Naghtan rules, a verdict which will normally lead to detainment in a "special" mental hospital. In trials for murder one may plead diminished responsibility on various grounds, including recognized mental disorders, and this, if successful, will lead to a conviction only for manslaughter. This may lead to compulsory hospitalization, imprisonment, or even to absolute discharge, as the court sees fit.

(e) The distinction between infanticide and murder represents, in effect, a recognition that a woman who has recently given birth may possess diminished responsibility for aggression against her baby.

The special defenses mentioned under (d) are now exceptional, and special treatment of the mentally abnormal person is primarily through methods (a), (b), and (c). All these are presumably to be regarded as cases where the anti-social person is treated rather than punished. If this is to be taken as implying that the people concerned are not held fully, or at all, to blame for what they did, then conviction cannot of itself be held to imply blameworthiness, a position which is rather unsatisfactory from the point of view of anyone who takes the notion of responsibility seriously, though he might admit its unavoidability in practice.

To the challenge sometimes put forth as to why the various restrictions on liberty implicit in compulsory treatment do not amount to punishment, the answer must surely be:

(i) that detainment in a hospital or medical treatment ends upon recovery, not after an amount of suffering or deprivation has been endured such as is deemed appropriate to the original offense;

(ii) that the unpleasantness of being thus detained is not a reason for the detainment;

(iii) that the detainment is not supposed to express "society's" disapproval of the individual on account of his behavior.

4d) Actions which followed inevitably in the given circumstances from a certain genetic endowment combined with certain environmental conditions.

So far as I know there is no legal system which countenances this in general terms as a ground for not punishing, though considerations included in this category may sometimes be taken as mitigating factors. Some might claim that our legal system implicitly incorporates the belief that the actions it renders punishable are not of this character. In any case there are those who hold that one cannot be rightly held morally responsible for such actions, some holding that all actions are of this character, and others denying it.

Acceptance of the principle of responsibility presumably implies that at least some of the circumstances enumerated above render punishment unfitting, but there can be considerable disagreement as to the interpretation and relevance of each of them. We shall shortly be considering the light in which such circumstances, and the principle itself, appear to certain distinct penological philosophies. But first I should like to consider certain grounds on which it might be argued that the law actually and rightly has little use for this principle in any case.

Law and Morality

It might be objected that the principle of moral responsibility, at least as we have presented it, incorporates a confusion between the scope of law and that of morality. It could be no objection to a law, it might be said, "that it penalizes those who may be morally innocent, since there is no necessary connection between legal and moral guilt,"[4] and this seems to imply that one may rightly be punished for an action to which no moral blame should attach. But a certain confusion is likely to arise here. Clearly, if any illegal actions are punishable at all, some are punishable which would not have been morally wrong if there had been no law against them. The view, held apparently by some eminent legal writers, that the criminal law exists only or primarily to punish acts which would be wrong in any case carries a moralistic view of law to an absurd extreme. Nonetheless, granted that an act's being forbidden by law entails a moral reason for desisting from it (though one which may sometimes be outweighed by other moral considerations), and granted, furthermore, that a law sets up expectations which it may be wrong to frustrate, it is arguable that in a well ordered country one should not be convicted of a criminal offense, or at least not be punished for it, without having done moral wrong. If, for instance, one considers it just that one should be punished for parking in a no parking area, does one not also think that one was morally at fault in doing so, however mild a moral wrong one may deem it? The issue is not, of course, whether immorality ever constitutes a sufficient condition of rightful punishment, only whether it is a necessary condition.

It is a real and important question how far one is morally justified in breaking a bad law, and one which carries with it the question how far the punishment of one who does so is morally just. One might hold that sometimes the offender was right to break the law and the judge also right in punishing him for doing so. Still, even if it may sometimes be the judge's duty thus to uphold a law which people are right to disobey, it presumably remains a bad thing that the morally innocent are being punished, and, in any case, there are surely limits to a judge's duty in this regard.

The complaint may still be made that our principle of responsibility confuses two different grounds on which a punishment might be rejected as wrong or excessive, the one resting on a denial of full personal responsibility (contra-indications 1 and 4, and perhaps 2), the other concerning the moral character of the act performed (contra-indication 3). It may even be claimed that to call someone personally responsible for an action simply is to say that he possessed normal consciousness of what he was doing and could have acted otherwise, and that this is a statement of fact, true or false, not of itself any kind of moral judgement at all, though it may become a ground for one.

However, the meaning to be attached in different contexts to the statement that someone could have acted otherwise than he did has been a subject of much philosophical controversy, and it seems beyond doubt that it may be true of a man that in one sense he could have done so, and in another not. If one asks which of these senses of "could have acted otherwise" is to be incorporated in the definition of personal responsibility, one is, in effect, trying to decide in what sense it is requisite that a man could have acted otherwise if he is to be blamed for an action that is considered objectionable. Thus the idea that, a man could have acted otherwise when it is used as a ground for regarding him as blameworthy for something, means only that he is, in some sense, responsible.

Certainly there appears to be a rather radical distinction between saying someone is not fully to blame for some harm he has done, because in the circumstances his action was morally excusable, and saying that he was not to blame because he could not help himself; but in many cases the distinction becomes rather thin. If I hand over the keys of a safe under the threat of death, there may be little real difference between my claiming forgiveness on the ground that I was too terrified to act otherwise, and on the ground that my choosing to survive was morally excusable. Upon the whole, then, it does not seem unreasonable to assemble all these cases together as contraindications of the moral responsibility widely though to be a necessary condition of rightful punishment.

Strict Liability

It has been a traditional principle of English law, and of law in all Common Law countries, that there is no offense without *mens rea*, without a guilty mind, that *actus non fecit reum nisi mens sit rea*. In some ways this goes further than our principle, for it demands a positively guilty intention, not merely a morally reprehensible lack of good intention.

It is sometimes claimed that the increase during this century of offenses for which liability is strict constitutes an erosion of this principle. Such an offense consists in the mere act, irrespective of whether the offender knew, or could have known, that the offense was being committed or could by any reasonable steps have prevented it. There seems to be disagreement in Britain now whether strict liability applies to statutory offenses where nothing implying the need for *mens rea* is specified, or whether the principle of *mens rea* applies wherever it has not been distinctly set aside.[5] Still, a typical and uncontroversial case where strict liability applies is the sale by a publican of intoxicating liquors to a minor, an intoxicated person, or a constable on duty, however unidentifiable as such they may be.

Regarding strict liability, we may make the following points.

1. It seems that in a fair number of cases what actually emerges from the treatment of an offense as one of strict liability is that a peculiarly high standard of care is demanded from persons in certain occupations. Once it is granted, as surely it ought to be, that one can be morally at fault through unintended negligence, it is arguable that a person punished for an offense of strict liability may have been morally at fault in terms of the peculiarly high standards of care the law has set up for him, even though he lacked *mens rea* properly speaking.[6]

2. Such an interpretation of the morality of strict liability is usually impossible, however, for even if it only applies where there exists a real opportunity on the part of the potential offender to reduce the chances of his offending, he may still offend in spite of all his efforts. The fact that such an offender is not to blame, on any serious criterion of blameworthiness, shows that English law does not, even in principle, conform wholly to the responsibility principle.

It would be a great mistake to conclude that the general spirit of English law is against our principle of responsibility. Not only do many lawyers object to the idea of strict liability, but, even when it is accepted, it is likely to be seen as overriding an important moral principle for special reasons, for example, the difficulty of obtaining proof that the offense was deliberate and the need to encourage especially high standards of care in certain trades. Moreover, the punishments in question are not normally severe and there is even some tendency to deny that they are punishments in the full sense of the word. We may note further that it has been well argued recently that the present direction of change, at least in Britain, is towards the reduction, not the increase, of strict liability.[7]

Retributivism

According to retributivism, as this theory is usually conceived, punishment is wrong where it is not deserved, and it is deserved only when a man's offense springs from moral failure, as it can do only if he could have acted otherwise, in the sense that his action arose from an act of free will of which there is no complete causal explanation, known or unknown, there being a general presumption that this is normally so.

There are various species of retributivism of which we shall mention three. 1) According to the first, a person ought not to be the happier for his immorality, and a main aim of punishment is to convert this "ought" into an "is". 2) According to the second, a state of affairs in which wrong doing results in a degree of suffering and disgrace somehow proportional thereto is intrinsically better than one in which wrong doing has no such consequence, and a main aim of punishment is artifically to establish such a causal relation. 3) A form of retributivism which enjoys more support today asserts that men normally have a right not to be subjected to the kind of suffering involved in punishment, but that this right is forfeited up to a limit, somehow determined by the degree of immorality, when a man, in his own immoral freedom, fails to respect the laws of his society. He can then be spoken of as deserving punishment, not in the sense that his immorality supplies a positive reason in itself for punishment, but in the sense that it gives society the right to punish him if this is deemed desirable for such ends as general or individual deterrence.

According to the first of these views, the punishment for an offense should be just about enough to make the offense on balance a source of unhappiness rather than happiness (a recommendation somewhat similar to that following from the simpler deterrence views, although on the latter the improbability of detection was supposed to give an additional ground for severity.) The other two views demand that the graver the offense the more severe the actual, or at least the maximum permissible, punishment. It should be obvious that all retributivists will accept the principle of responsibility, and the relevance, in principle, of each of our contra-indications.

Although retributivist views are now rare among penologists, the grounds for rejecting them seem sometimes to rest on acceptance of one rather dubious component thereof. We are told sometimes that no offender is really morally responsible for his failings, because these are the inevitable product of the bad conditioning to which he has been subject, or to other factors over which he had no control, and that *therefore* retributive punishment is misplaced. This implies that there might have been such a thing as free will (but scientific evidence points away from this), and that if there had been, retributive punishment would have been in order. In opposition to this view, I would urge, first, that no one has given a sufficiently intelligible account of free will for it to make sense either to suppose that there might be such a thing, or that it has any particular moral implications, and, secondly, that the essential retributivist position is logically independent of any belief **in free will.**

One can say that, for an action to be, in part, the product of free will, there must be nothing in the past circumstances or in the present nature of the agent which completely explains why he chose to act as he did. So far as these go, the agent might have chosen to do either A or B. What then does explain why he chose to do A rather than B? Answer: the choice was an act of free will. The trouble is that the same answer would apply had he chosen B, and therefore does not explain his choice of A instead. The honest answer, then, is that there is no explanation of his having chosen A. Even if there are factors which made it more probable that he would choose A, the free-will-ist must say that there is no explanation of why he made the more rather than the less probable choice, since he must hold that both were possible.

Now there is no essential difficulty in allowing that some events have no explanation, but that there is an element of randomness at the heart of things. What is difficult is to see why choices which are without explanation should somehow merit blame or punishment in a sense in which explicable choices do not. Schopenhauer seems to have been essentially right in holding that the idea that a man could have acted otherwise makes sense if you mean that the act sprang from his choice and would not have occured without it, but it does not make sense if you mean that he could have chosen otherwise. I would add that this is not because we know that every choice is determined, but because even if undetermined it is quite unclear what is meant by saying that it might have been otherwise, (unless you mean merely that this is logically conceivable — and that is equally true of determined choices, since causal laws are not logically necessary). Thus the whole idea of "could have chosen to act otherwise" as opposed to "could, or would, have acted otherwise, if he had chosen" seems to lack any genuine content. This is a very old argument, and in view of some modern discussions of it, ought to be treated at greater length, but it still seems to me essentially right.

To link retributivism with free will is to link a very natural human attitude with a form of words to which no clear meaning can be attached. I suggest that logically the two are quite independent, and that retributivism is really a view about the proper response to an evil will as such, whatever the explanation of its existence. We may well reject the view, but our rejection cannot properly be based on a denial of free will.

When retributivism is freed from its confusing entanglement with a doctrine of free will, its commitment to the principle of responsibility is not lessened. The only contra-indication which will lose its relevance is 4d) and even then, a good deal of what tends to be presented under this head might find a home elsewhere. Blame, it will be held, is the judgement that an action sprang from a genuine choice of evil together with a consequent emotion of hostility towards the agent, and punishment is essentially the socially organized and controlled manifestation of this hostility. Retributivism regards a man's will as the central essence of his being and feels that resentment, anger, etc. should only be directed at wrongful willing. Blame and punishment are therefore out of place whenever an offense does not spring from the offender's will to evil, and this is something which contra-indications 1), 2), 3) and 4a) all go to establish.

We should perhaps add that a retributivist may regard a man as blameable for an action which manifests a will too little directed at the good of others, even if not positively directed at evil. Retributivist jurists have tended to insist on the need for positive *mens rea* as an ingredient of criminality and have therefore disliked the treatment of mere negligence as criminal. However, I suggest that retributivism, and indeed common morality, would not really think blame appropriate for a failure to concern oneself with the needs of others unless this has at some stage arisen from not bothering to do things which one at least dimly recognized the desirability of doing.

The real problem for the retributivist, as indeed for most other theorists, regards the importance and interpretation of contra-indications 4b and 4c. Yet the general nature of his outlook upon the problem is clear enough. He only blames those whose actions reflect, more or less directly, a real choice of evil. He will thus regard as exculpatory anything which shows that the agent lacked a moral sense, and thus he can regard certain types of psychopaths as blameless in the sense in which cats are blameless for their cruelty to birds. The retributivist will also, though this is more problematic, regard as at least partially exculpatory those impulses which take control of a man in spite of intense efforts to resist them, where it seems appropriate to regard the effort to resist as representing the true person and the impulse as an alien force. As to when this is appropriate, it might depend on the extent to which the agent identifies himself for the most part with one or other aspect of his personality. If, for instance, he has seriously sought medical aid to assist his control of the impulse, this suggests that his main personality regards it as something alien and that he is to be counted as its opponent along with the agents of law enforcement. The question "Could he have tried harder?" is of doubtful meaning; the question whether he tried hard to resist the impulse with hostility is much more straightforward. If we say a man did his best to resist an impulse, we mean that his resistance came up to a standard we regard as reasonable or even noble. Finally, the retributivist will clearly agree with the M'Naghten rules regarding the blamelessness of those whose ignorance of the nature or illegality of what they did reflects no deliberate evil doing but a lack of ordinary cognitive ability.

The "No Responsibility" View

Retributivism is the theory which will lay most emphasis on the issue of moral responsibility when it comes to the disposing of offenders. So let us now turn to the other extreme and consider the view that the issue of moral responsibility should not be raised in this connection at all. Lady Wootton's advocacy of this view is among the most discussed and doubtless among the most influential, and it is her argument that I shall take as an example of such a view.

According to her[8] the attempt to decide whether an offender is morally responsible or not is both impossible and pointless. It is impossible because, as she interprets the question, it means that we ask such questions as: "Could the offender have resisted this impulse?" Such questions are unanswerable because there is no empirical way of distinguishing between an impulse which was merely not resisted and one which could not have been. It is pointless because we should no longer be thinking along retributivist lines and trying to make people suffer in proportion to their moral guilt. Rather, we should be seeking simply for measures which, without being inhumane, are likely to prevent him from offending again.

Lady Wootton proposes, therefore, that the court should set for itself simply and solely the task of deciding whether the accused committed the offense, and that all issues of *mens rea*, of sanity, and so forth, should be set aside, and that the verdict should concern this and nothing else. Then, if it is once established that the accused did commit the offense, he should be subjected to treatment which primarily on the basis of the best statistical evidence, seems least likely to be followed by a repetition. There will be no need ever to decide on whether people are mad or bad, sick or at moral fault.

There is great appeal in such a view. Surely it puts the question of the disposal of offenders on the right basis in regarding the prevention of further offenses as the primary aim. All the same, there are aspects of Lady Wootton's view which may well be disturbing upon reflection.

An offender subjected to the treatment judged most likely to effect an improvement in his behavior would have no clear ground for complaining that the severity of his sentence was out of proportion to his offense. Certainly Lady Wootton is careful to point out that there are moral limitations upon the methods we could be justified in using to prevent anti-social behavior, but for her these could hardly include the fact that a punishment was undeserved. If the considerations which might make us use this term are allowed moral relevance under a different description (as is perhaps likely), then the issue of moral responsibility would itself, in effect, arise again in different terms. If it did not, then there is little doubt that some "sentences," or modes of treatment, would rightly be recommended from her point of view even though such treatment would strike many of us as unjust, especially when based on statistically indicated "prediction tables." It would be difficult, for instance, to discountenance measures directed not only at the prevention of further offenses of the same kind, but at the prevention of other sorts of offenses which persons of the same type, left untreated, might be expected eventually to commit. Or suppose, to take a quite imaginary possibility that in the case of those who had been to universities no significant difference in reconviction rates were found between those who were imprisoned for a certain type of offense and those who were given an absolute discharge; but that when similar groups who had been to colleges of technology were studied, reconviction rates were significantly lower for the imprisoned group. Should we feel happy at drawing the conclusion that, of two such persons engaged jointly in such an offense, the one should therefore be imprisoned and the other not, or should we not feel that this was unjust? Certainly the individuation of sentences, so that they suit the offender and not merely the offense, is acceptable when it relates to individual culpability, but this is something rather different. How do we feel, for instance, when we learn that, according to the (British) *Children and Young Persons Act 1969*, if two children between ten and fourteen commit an offense, and one is thought to come from a good home and the other from a bad home, only the latter can be brought before the court? Anything of this sort applied to adults would certainly shock us, yet it could follow from the Wootton approach.

Do such objections represent an unthinking moral conservatism, or can they be supported within an intelligent moral framework? Professor Hart has made some telling points in this connection, arguing that it is personal responsibility, the having had the opportunity to avoid clashes with the law, not the moral responsibility or blameworthiness of the retributivists which matters.[9] The point of making personal responsibility an ingredient of crime, he argues, is that this leaves the citizen the choice of breaking the law and being punished to an extent roughly predictable or keeping the law and being free of the unpleasanter sort of interference.

There is a great deal to be said for such an argument, but I doubt that it is wholly adequate. In spite of his disclaimers, Hart's account makes punishment very much like a tax on conduct, such as a purchase tax on cigarettes designed to discourage smoking, and plays down the disgrace punishment is supposed to carry. One might say that, for Hart, the offender chooses punishment rather than is punished for his choice. It is unclear precisely in what sense the rightly punished offender must have had the *opportunity* to avoid his clash with society. Certainly some who choose crime and thereby the risk of punishment find any other course of life so unattractive that for them society is as restrictive of the only liberty they wish to enjoy as Wootton's world would be for others.

Another familiar objection to the Wootton approach is that it might justify radical assaults upon the personality of offenders by surgical, chemical, or psychological techniques. "If an anti-social person can be changed by medical treatment into a well-conducted citizen, it is only common sense that he should be so treated."[10] Such remarks may well have a chilling effect, especially if we think of offenses which have a political character.[11] It is true that Lady Wootton emphasizes the existence of moral limits to the permissible types of treatment, but one may feel that as yet none have been formulated which are not closely entwined with the traditional idea of responsibility.

The objection I shall press against Lady Wootton's "no responsibility" view, however, is of a different nature and concerns the readiness to detach the other features of punishment from those which connect it with desert. We are told that " . . . a sentencing policy which makes the prevention of crime its primary objective is not necessarily to be equated with one that is 'soft'. Such a policy is non-punitive in the sense that it neither regards punishment as an end in itself nor evaluates crimes and those who commit them in terms of what each is thought to deserve. But, while adhering to the rule of minimum action, it does not rule out the use of penalties or discard deterrence altogether . . . "[12]

But is it possible or desirable, one may ask, to retain deterrent measures, whose unpleasantness is not incidental but of their essence, (*fines* are a very pure example), while eliminating any sense on the part of the public that it is a disgrace to undergo them? If such measures are to remain disgraceful, then they are expressive of blame, and their application should be proportional to the degree of blame which is appropriate. If Lady Wootton replies that disgrace should come only to those whose disgrace serves a socially useful function, then it should be recalled that many philosophers have identified such persons with those who can properly be called morally responsible. There are, after all, alternatives to the retributivist view regarding the nature of blameworthiness, and the decision as to who should be subjected to measures expressive of society's disapproval cannot be separated from the question of the proper objects of such disapproval. It is true that in point of fact restriction in a mental hospital carries its own kind of stigma. All the same, part of the point of denying someone's moral responsibility on grounds of mental disease is, surely, to establish that his behavior should not invite blame, that is, resentment, anger, and the attempt to make him ashamed of himself; and most would therefore agree that the stigma attaching to mental illness is regrettable. Should we likewise make an effort to remove all disgrace and social stigma from deterrent measures akin to our present punishments? This is probably neither feasible nor desirable. It would be very hard to impose deterrent sentences if these did not serve, among other things, to express society's resentment at certain forms of conduct. Thus, at least so long as such measures are judged effective, the question of moral responsibility seems bound to remain in some form.

The Deterrent Theory and Moral Responsibility

When punishment is defended by those who do not accept that retribution is an end in itself, it is usually on grounds of deterrence, whether general (i.e., of other potential offenders) or individual (i.e., of the offender himself). Some indeed defend punishment as an instrument of reformation, but, though there is a genuine conceptual difference between individual deterrence and reform, the two are not easily distinguished in practice, and we may conveniently group them together as a single aim. (This only applies to the reform which is reputed to come from the shame of being punished; reform arising from measures incidental to the punishment as such is a different matter.)

The present theory differs from Lady Wootton's in the emphasis it puts upon general deterrence. She has argued that it is much easier to establish the utility of different modes of treating offenders from the point of view of individual deterrence and reform than it is to discover their utility as instruments of general deterrence, and that sentencing policy should be based mainly upon the former consideration.[13] One might reply that it is scarcely practicable to take no steps at all, on the basis of general theory or even "common sense," on matters where statistical evidence is slight. In any case it is difficult to believe that a policy directed only at improving the offending individual's behavior would be rational. Would it be sensible even to try paying offenders large sums of money not to repeat their offenses, or are we not justified on grounds of common sense in supposing that a whole class of new offenders would thereby be brought into existence? However that may be, the standard deterrent theorist holds that punishment can be effective both as an individual and general deterrent, and that the penal system should be directed at the protection of society at the least cost in actual punishments imposed, and never at a cost outweighing the harm which would otherwise spring from the offenses. The question for us is the implications of such a theory for the principle of responsibility.

Traditional deterrence theorists have attempted to show that those who can be described as not to blame for their offenses are all offenders of a category for whom punishment as a deterrent is either useless or unnecessary. It can be argued, fairly convincingly, that each of our contra-indications except 4d (which would be disallowed) can be interpreted as indicative of this. Still there are difficulties. It would seem to follow, for one thing, that the regular recidivist is not responsible. This might be accepted, however, and such measures of protection as society takes against him might be distinguished from punishment proper (as preventive detention was supposed to be at one time).

Professor Hart, however,[14] has urged that there is a basic logical flaw in this approach, since there is no guarantee that there may not be categories of individually undeterrable offenders whose punishment is useful as a general deterrent at what the deterrence theorist should count an acceptable cost, e.g., those suffering from mental diseases which others can simulate. He admits that the most economical mode of general deterrence may be one in which none are punished but those for whom individual deterrence is in order, but he claims that most of us attach an importance to some principle of responsibility greater that this mere possibility or probability would warrant.

On the other hand, however, it may be that by taking a somewhat "higher ground" a defense of the principle of responsibility can be given which is consonant with a broadly deterrent view. This defense will rest mainly upon a certain theory of blame, or adverse moral judgement, according to which, justified blame is liable to include three main factors.

(1) First, one forms a certain opinion of the state of *will* expressed in the conduct blamed, and this opinion carries with it a certain sentiment or feeling regarding the state of will. Whatever may be said of the sentiment, the opinion has a certain degree of truth in a comparatively straightforward sense; the degree of concern that an individual has for the good of others, for example, is essentially a matter of fact.

(2) Secondly, one may communicate this opinion or sentiment towards the person blamed, and this may have certain effects, inasmuch as the ordinary moral agent will dislike this, not simply because he dislikes others thinking that he is to blame, but because he dislikes being forced to recognize that the opinion is true. Shame, regret, and repentance consist essentially in such melancholy recognition, and in the healthy mind they assist towards a modification of the will which renders the objectionable description less apt.

(3) Thirdly, the formulation of this opinion normally plays a part in modifying or sustaining characteristics of the critic's own will and, likewise, of the will of those who participate in his criticism. One's recognition of the undesirability of certain states of will, and of the ease with which they can develop, acts as a check to their development within oneself. Of course, in the case of self-blame, the second and third factors collapse into one.

By and large one may say that sentiments and opinions are not moral unless they concern the will, and either themselves have, or are intimately related to sentiments and opinions which have, effects of types 2 and 3.

What is in question is more than the will of which the agent is conscious, which has become an object of attention, but it is not more than the will which consists in states of consciousness. One may not be conscious of one's dislike of someone, yet one's dislike of him may consist partly in such things as the way his face looks to one, the way his voice sounds, the emotional tinge to the way one experiences news about him, all of which are states, without necessarily being objects, of consciousness. Impulses which emerge from the unconscious only in moments of bizarre activity, without having been previously present even as an unacknowledged aspects of one's consciousness, seem rather forces which impinge from outside, than aspects of the personality which we can criticize morally, if only because such criticism (it seems) could not have consequences in the individual of the kind we have indicated.

There are persons for whom the adverse moral judgement of their neighbors cannot have the effects mentioned in (2), at least insofar as a certain aspect of their will is concerned. It may be that they cannot be brought to see themselves in the relevant light, or it may be that the relevant aspect of their personality cannot be modified by their thus seeing themselves. I shall say that such persons do not belong to the inner moral community, or a least to the inner moral community of those in relation to whose moral criticism they are so described, meaning that moral criticism is wasted so far as they are concerned.

Yet among those who do not belong to the inner moral community there may be some such that those who do so might become akin to them if they allow themselves, or are allowed, to become neglectful of the demands of morality, and who themselves have moved further away from the moral community because this was allowed to happen in their case. The moral criticism of such persons can have the effects mentioned in (3), and I shall say that they belong to the outer circle of the moral community.

According to the position I am describing, actions are only blameworthy insofar as they express the conscious will (in the more inclusive sense of "conscious") and insofar as the persons concerned belong, in respect to that aspect of the will, to the inner or outer moral community. Only in those cases does moral blame fulfill what, for such theorists, is its proper function — the preservation of certain standards regarding the proper objects of endeavor and the permissible ways of attaining them.

If a wife criticizes her husband for being selfish in certain matters, and if the husband sees the justice of such criticism, he may dislike recognizing this truth about himself and may be affected for the good. But there comes a time when a person is so settled in habits of selfishness that such a result is ruled out. All the same, those who identify a person as being selfish and therefore judge him adversely may be digesting the fact that this is what one can easily become unless an effort is made. On the other hand, there are people, including those we might call psychopathic, whose disregard for others stems from a general state of the personality which no member of the inner moral community is ever likely to fall into, unless perhaps as a result of physical changes against which a lively sense of moral values is no check. To say that such people lack moral responsibility and are not to blame need not damage our sensitivity to moral demands, for we know that we do not risk becoming like *that* by moral complacency or backsliding.

It may be argued that to blame people who, in respect of what they are blamed for, do not belong even to the larger moral community may still serve to uphold moral standards, since people's discriminations are not that subtle. This is akin to a point of Professor Hart's we discussed above regarding the deterrence theory of punishment.

The answer to this argument varies somewhat with the type of case. Where a man is not morally responsible for an action because it sprang from an aspect of his personality normally deeply submerged in the unconscious, calling him morally responsible expresses a false opinion and threatens all the values involved in the respect for truth. We have already indicated one reason why moral criticism should, by definition, concern only the conscious will, but we may add that it is deeply embedded in our notion of what a person essentially is. But what of a vicious psychopath whose brutal purposes may be essential elements in his conscious will? The answer surely is that we may feel what aversion we like towards him, but that since he is not the sort of person normal moral agent risks becoming, it is better that we be taught to realize this truth and contrast his personality traits with those against which conscientious feelings are enlisted to battle.

There is a traditional utilitarian-empiricist account of blame to which ours is related, but with which it should not be confused. According to that account, blame is, in effect, a conditioned negative reinforcer, associated perhaps with punishment in childhood or with withdrawal of affection, whose proper use, like punishment, is as an individual and general deterrent. Our view holds, in contrast, that to blame is not a mere means by which we seek to control each other, but an opinion and an ensuing sentiment, and that even its effect upon the person blamed need not spring merely from his wish to be liked but may owe more to the departure from his own ideal which he is forced to recognize. The detached observer of society may quite properly see the whole business of moral criticism as a means of mutual social control and as valuable only in so far as socially useful, but the opinions expressed in the actual process of moral criticism need to be true if serious and damaging misunderstandings of human personality are not to be created.

Turning back now to the issue of punishment and to our principle of responsibility, I suggest that if the deterrence theorist is inclined to give support to this principle, on grounds stronger than those criticized by Professor Hart, it is because, in effect, he does not think of punishment merely as a form of unpleasantness which people are anxious to avoid, but as a mark of disgrace attached to the offender and his offense. He accepts the view, apt to be urged by judges and to be derided by philosophers, that punishment, among other things, is "the emphatic denunciation by the community of a crime."[15] That is, he sees punishment as, in part, an extension of the practice of moral criticism and as a reinforcement of the community's moral standards, including the principle that laws should be obeyed. It is certainly arguable that the idea of punishment as an expression of blame, the mode in which the community acts towards those with whom it feels that it has the right to be angry, is so essential to the notion summoned up by the term "punishment" that even if there were deterrent measures which did not include the aspect of blame they could not properly be called punishment. Could a judge, on passing a penal sentence say, without oddity, "I do not blame you for what you have done, but a spell in prison (or whatever) may discourage you and others from acting thus again"? Subjecting to the stigma of punishment those in whom the creation of shame for their action is either pointless or impossible and whom the mass of persons run no risk of becoming like through a weakening of their moral sense, is attaching blame in its strongest form where it is false as an opinion and will have neither of the two types of consequences which give point to the attachment of blame.

Acceptance of the principle of responsibility on these grounds represents a qualification of, rather than a deduction from, a deterrence theory of punishment, but not one alien to its essential spirit. After all, those who justify punishment as a means of reducing crime are unlikely to deny that, in forwarding this end, its crudely deterrent effect is intertwined with its general reinforcement of the community's sense of right and wrong by the blame-expressing stigma it attaches to certain actions and that to deprive punishment of this blame-expressing role, and hence of the limitations upon its use which this imposes (unless we circumvent them by deceit, something objectionable on many grounds), would leave a morally sterilized system of threats of greatly reduced effectiveness. This whole point of view would admittedly break down if it could be shown that all criminal offenders lie outside the moral community in the sense we have described, but although I would admit and even insist that many more do fall outside it than are recognized in current pratices, it remains at least very likely that the ordinary law abiding citizen might well become an offender if his conscientious feelings were allowed to decline too far.

A deterrence theory thus qualified will have a place which should be sufficiently clear for the main contra-indications of moral responsibility we have listed, and it will suggest guidelines for those who attempt to make them more precise. Contra-indications 1-4a mainly attest to the comparative innocence of the will, if any, behind the deed. The contra-indications which concern mental disorder or abnormality are, of course, much more problematic, but the general principle would be that objectionable actions springing from dispositions against which moral feelings are no defense — either because it is of their essence to exclude their development (some cases of 4c) or for the very different reason that their presence in strength would provide no effective check (other cases of 4c and of 4b) — are not proper objects of blame. The problem of distinguishing between an impulse which is irresistible and one which is simply not resisted becomes that of distinguishing between actions against which the moral sense of the community is no defense and those against which it is; and one may urge that the best evidence of a deed's springing from an impulse of the former kind is that the agent shows evidence of a real moral struggle to resist.

We have already suggested that no rational view can make 4d, in and of itself, a ground of blamelessness, but this is not to say that there may not be some considerations about an individual's childhood or adult environment which diminish responsibility. There may, for instance, be degrees of under-privilege in which the considerations which should lead most of us to refrain from crimes of dishonesty have a very diminished applicability. Such cases are really contra-indications of type 3 but they may masquerade as cases of 4d, thus seeming to confirm the idea that 4d is a legitimate type of contra-indication in itself. Of course, a judgement of blamelessness thus based will reflect a radical critique of the society of which the court is an agent, and it is therefore only to a very limited extent that the court can reaonably be expected to take such a critique into account. A judge can hardly honorably retain his position if he thinks his society is so unjust that there are moral agents who do no wrong in disobeying its laws. The most one can expect is that such factors may serve in mitigation of the offense when sentence is passed.

One might also urge as an implication of our account of blame that it is only appropriate where blamer and blamed belong to the same moral community, and that since many offenders grow up in a sub-culture with its own minority moral standards, they are not proper objects of blame by the rest of us. This consideration, pressed home, might drastically reduce the number of serious offenders whom we should consider it right to stigmatize as deserving punishment rather than as requiring re-education or non-punitive control or "treatment."

Of course, the different contra-indications of moral responsibility differ greatly in their implications. In removing or mitigating blameworthiness they may or may not show that society has more to fear from the offender. The mentally sick, and possibly the morally under-educated, may need compulsory treatment or control. We are not now concerned with the moral limitations upon such methods, but only with the point that they should be distinguished from punishment, even if by any chance they should contain an element of deterrence. Compulsory treatment, and even deterrence, of the non-responsible may or may not be unpleasant, but it seems right to distinguish it from punishment (where, for instance, Lady Wootton would blur the distinction) inasmuch as it does not reflect an adverse moral judgement upon the recipient's conduct. I have tried to show that the essential idea behind a deterrence view of punishment is compatible with insistence upon this distinction and with the criteria of moral responsibility which go with it.

Of the three theories of punishment I have discussed, retributivism, "no responsibility," and deterrence qualified by the principle of moral responsibility, I can safely say that I reject the first, as it stands in isolation, but would point out that much of it is taken up and given a rational foundation by a theory such as the third. The second is appealing, but must be rejected unless we are prepared either to jettison the notion of anyone ever being blameworthy, or to say that all offenders against the law stand in such a separate category from the rest of us that the issue of blameworthiness should not be raised in their case, and I doubt whether either of these is really acceptable. Of the third, in its final version, I think we may say at least this — that to the extent that punishment is a proper response to crime, then it is because something like this theory holds. It certainly seems doubtful whether we can afford to dispense with the view that at least some law breakers, even if less of them than is commonly held, are to blame for their offenses and that this needs to be insisted on. It may be, however, that we should insist upon this more in other ways, for instance, by putting greater emphasis on reparations. What I hope we may agree upon, at least, is that so long as punishment exists, the principle of responsibility should be respected.

NOTES

[1] References to current legal and penal practices will be concerned primarily with Britain throughout, though I must disclaim any very adequate grasp of the situation even here.

[2] For a useful account of this see *Law and Psychiatry* by S. Glueck (1963) Chapter III.

[3] See *Crime and Punishment in Britain* by Nigel Walker (1968 edition) Chapter 13.

[4] *Criminal Responsibility* by F. G. Jacobs (1971) p. 129.

[5] *Op. cit.*, pp. 111 et ff; also pp. 97-98.

[6] Lord Devlin spoke of punishment for "thoughtlessness or inefficiency" in this connection in a judgement quoted on p. 113 of Jacobs-*op. cit.*

[7] *Op. cit.*, Chapter 4. For the contrary view see *Crime and the Criminal Law* by Barbara Wootton.

[8] *Crime and the Criminal Law* by Barbara Wootton (1963); also the same author's *Science and Social Pathology* (1959) esp. chapters VII and VIII.

⁹Cf. *Punishment and Responsibility* by H. L. A. Hart pp. 180-185, and elsewhere, especially essay II. Of course, there is far more to Hart's argument than can be indicated here.

¹⁰*Social Science and Social Pathology* p. 252.

¹¹Lady Wooton is, of course, one of those who has especially emphasized the danger of regarding unpopular opinions as symptoms of illness, but this hardly annuls the point that punitive methods are not directed at the essence of the person as "treatment" might be and therefore are less of a threat to the social rebel's right to think for himself.

¹²*Crime and the Criminal Law* p. 116.

¹³*Crime and the Criminal Law* p. 101.

¹⁴*Punishment and Responsibility* by H. L. A. Hart pp. 18-21.

¹⁵Evidence of Lord Denning to the *Royal Commission on Capital Punishment* quoted in Hart-*Op. cit.* p. 170. The view that this is the main point of punishment is not, however, the one of our concern.

GERTRUDE EZORSKY
Punishment and Excuses

Most modern legal philosophers regard strict liability — the denial of legal excuses — as morally unattractive. Why is this so? Consider that, if a defendant is strictly liable, no standard legal excuse, i.e., insanity, ignorance or mistake of fact, coercion, necessity, incompetence or automatism, can be accepted as a defense. Thus, if a careful driver kills a child, who, without warning, darts in front of his car, the driver would be convicted. A defendant who could prove that heroin, discovered in his home, had been hidden there by the former owner would be punished. A father, who, under serious threat of murder to his family, stored a thief's takings, would be convicted for receiving stolen goods.

Is it not obvious that legal excuses improve the moral quality of life? So it seems. But I shall argue that under some circumstances (to be specified) offenders should be strictly liable to punishment.

The kind of punishment under consideration is imprisonment, i.e., confinement in a prison, not the torture or degrading treatment which, as a matter of fact, is practiced in at least some penal institutions.

Without Fault?

Let us take a close moral look at our luckless, strictly liable offender. He violated the law but has some standard legal excuse. However, in his case, a standard legal excuse is not accepted as a defense.

How shall we mark the manner of his misdoing?

> Where X is done in circumstances such that, if X were legally prohibited, the agent would have some standard legal excuse for doing X, let X be called involuntary. Where X is involuntary, and is in fact prohibited by law, let X be called an involuntary offense. Where X is not done in circumstances such that X is involuntary, let X be called voluntary.

Involuntary offenders are legally guilty but morally innocent, i.e., without fault.

Are such persons really without fault? Richard Wasserstrom suggests that at least some involuntary offenders may, in a "sense," be at fault. He cites the case of *State* v. *Lindberg*, in which the defendent, a bank director, involuntarily violated a statute governing loans by bank officers. (The violation occurred, presumably, because Lindberg had been misinformed about the transaction by another bank official.)

As Wasserstrom sees the matter, Lindberg might, in a sense, have been at fault here, since

> ... there was a conscious intent to engage in just that activity — banking — which the defendant *knew, or should have known* to be subject to criminal sanctions if certain consequences ensued. And there was a still clearer intent to do the more specific act — borrow money — which the defendant *knew or should have known* to be subject to criminal sanctions under certain specified circumstances.[1] (emphasis added)

Of course, defendants who merely "should have" known, but didn't know, that their acts were "subject to criminal sanctions" are at fault. They are, at least, negligent with respect to knowledge of the law, hence plainly at fault. But Wasserstrom also suggests that defendants who are not even negligent may be at fault. Let us generalize his suggestion:

The following condition is to be known as *risk* and suffices to establish fault for involuntary offenses:

> B is a legally prohibited act. The agent knows that, if in doing A voluntarily he does B involuntarily, his excuse for doing B would not be accepted as a defense against criminal sanctions.
>
> The agent in doing A voluntarily does B involuntarily.

According to Wasserstrom's suggestion, where *risk* obtains, the agent may, in some sense, be at fault. But I deny that *risk* ever suffices to establish fault (in any sense). Here is why: consider the hypothetical cases of D and N, both druggists. Each was convicted for violating a strict liability law prohibiting sale, without a written order, of substances containing narcotics. *Risk* held in both cases.

D is scrupulously careful to obey the law. He double checks all prescriptions, never leaves stock unattended, etc. However, a competitor,

C, succeeds in an ingenious plot to get D imprisoned. C distracts the truck driver who is delivering cough syrup to D, while C's confederate substitutes identical bottles of syrup spiked with narcotics. D receives the spiked syrup and innocently sells it. C sees to it that legal authorities discover the sale and D goes to trial. C's confederate confesses to the plot. D is nevertheless convicted. According to law, he is strictly liable, hence the excuse, ignorance of fact, in unacceptable as a defense.

N's story is quite different. He buys a drug store from a crooked druggist who had sold falsely labelled substances containing narcotics. N knows his predecessor's history, but, lackadaisical fellow that he is, fails to carefully analyse the contents of the bottles he finds on the shelves. He just sniffs the contents and decides they're okay. However, one of the bottles contains sniff-proof narcotics. N sells it to an unsuspecting customer and is subsequently charged and convicted. His excuse, ignorance of fact, is not accepted as a defense.

Since *risk* obtained in both cases, both D and N knew that, if in voluntarily selling drugs they involuntarily sold, without a written order, a substance containing narcotics, then a standard legal excuse would not be accepted as a defense against criminal sanctions. Thus, if as Wasserstron suggests, *risk* suffices for fault, then both druggists are at fault. But I claim that only N, the sniffing druggist, is at fault. His sniff test simply falls short of reasonably care. We need not hypothesize any special "sense" of fault to establish N's fault. Plainly, he failed to do something he should have done — make a careful analysis of the bottles he found on his shelves. N was either negligent or reckless, hence, at fault. Since he had an excuse (ignorance of fact), he is less culpable than a voluntary offender. However, this excuse only reduces, but does not eliminate, his fault.[2]

D, however, exercised scrupulous care, taking every reasonable precaution to obey the law. There is no act or omission which would have prevented his offense that D should have performed, but didn't. In that case, I submit, he is not at fault. What can he be faulted for? Doing A, i.e., selling drugs? Of course not. If D shouldn't sell drugs, neither should anyone else.

Whenever an agent is at fault for involuntarily committing a prohibited act, then there is some act or omission which he should have performed, but didn't. In all such cases, the agent is, like N, our sniffing druggist, either reckless or negligent. D, however, was neither.

Hence, I suggest, he was not at fault. Since *risk* held in his case, then **D** did know beforehand that he might be subject to legal sanctions. But *what* he knew, in so knowing, was that through *no fault of his own* **he** might be punished. Thus, against the accusation that he was at fault, D would have every reason to protest, "what should I have done that I failed to do?"

Assumptions

In what follows, I shall argue that, under specified circumstances, an involuntary offender should, despite his blamelessness, be punished. My argument, however, does not justify punishing the offender who, in addition to his blamelessness, has a further, distinct sort of moral complaint. For example, suppose his punishment would be interpreted by the community as proof of fault. In that case he has two different items of complaint. First, he is punished, though blameless. Second, society is deceived in thinking him at fault. My argument, however, merely justifies punishing some blameless offenders. I am not arguing that any blameless offender ought to be punished, if, as a consequence of punishment he would be falsely stigmatized as blameworthy. Hence it will be useful to restrict our cases to those involuntary offenders who are generally known to be blameless. We shall assume that the community would not be deceived by their punishment into believing them to be at fault.

Our no deception assumption is exemplified in such cases as these: a careful driver is lawfully convicted for involuntarily running over a child, although everyone knows he is blameless. A military commander is publically humiliated — stripped of his rank and sentenced to imprisonment — for losing a battle. Yet everyone who knows of his punishment is perfectly aware that he was not at fault.

The no deception assumption will be coupled with a second stipulation: *Risk* holds in all involuntary offenses to be considered. Here is why: Consider a person who is made to suffer a loss by legal means, e.g., taxation, quarantine or imprisonment. Suppose he was not given due legal notice that he might be so treated, or could not assimilate such notice, e.g., he is feeble minded. In either case he is the victim of a distinct type of unfairness, which we may call a failure of due notice. Why is such failure unfair? When an individual is duly warned, he may, wherever possible, adjust his activity accordingly. A taxpayer forewarned, can whittle down his spending. A potential strict liability offender, so warned, might reduce the probability of punishment by super caution or by giving up his legally perilous enterprise, e.g., a druggist might sell his business rather than risk an undeserved prison sentence.

Where *risk* fails, the involuntary offender has been deprived of due notice. But I am not claiming that any blameless offender who has been so deprived should be punished. Let us then exclude any such irrelevant case by assuming that *risk* holds for all our involuntary offenders.

Note then that our offenders knew, in advance, the conditions of liability. Hence my argument does not apply to those involuntary offenders who could not assimilate such knowledge, e.g., to the feeble minded or to the deluded megalomaniac who is incapable of believing, hence incapable of knowing, that *he* is subject to penal sanctions.

Our two assumptions — no deception and *risk* — are exemplified in all involuntary offenses to be considered herewith. Given these assumptions about our offender, we can focus our undistracted moral intuition on the fact which interest us — the fact of his faultlessness.

The two assumptions have a further useful purpose. They serve to relevantly distinguish our blameless offenders from those who suffer other varieties of undeserved punishment. Those punished retroactively are not given due notice by law. Victims of illegal police frameups are not so forewarned, nor are they usually free from a false stigma of blame. Hence my argument should not be construed to bear on such cases.

However, at least some vicarious victims of punishment, i.e., those punished for the offense of another, do relevantly resemble our involuntary offenders. A careful, cautious parent, vicariously convicted for his child's offense, can, like our careful cautious druggist, D, be forewarned and known to be blameless. Indeed, as we shall see, the argument which might send D to prison can lock up this parent as well.

Let us turn now to the views of philosophers on this matter of strict liability.

Utilitarianism

Utilitarians proclaim the glory of human happiness and the evil of human misery. We are enjoined to maximize human happiness and minimize human suffering. Why, then, should any sort of punishment (itself a misery) be justified on a utilitarian appraisal?

Utilitarians have argued that legal punishment has at least one good consequence — persons who aspire to crime are deterred by the threat of punishment. Is this claim true? Let us state this deterrence claim in the following modest fashion: It is reasonable to believe that the threat of punishment effectively deters at least some who might otherwise succumb to crime. Moreover, in at least some cases, punishment achieves a greater gain in utility than other feasible alternatives. In such cases utilitarians should opt for laws prescribing punishment of criminals.

Can punishment of involuntary offenders serve the purpose of deterrence? Bentham insisted that such punishment is useless. "Where the will cannot be deterred . . . punishment must be inefficacious."[3] Let us see.

Notice first that strict liability may be either total or specific. The total variety holds in a legal system where all offenders are strictly liable, while the specific sort obtains when offenders against some laws, but not all, are strictly liable.

Total strict liability would most certainly be a utilitarian nightmare. Consider a legal system where ignorance of the nature or consequences of one's act gave no protection against punishment. The postal employees who unknowingly assist a bomb through the mail, the waiter who in innocent ignorance serves poisoned coffee; they, together with the vast multitudes who unknowingly contribute causally to crime, would all be implicated and punished as accessories. If a whole community unknowingly committed the offense of passing a counterfeit bill, everyone would land in jail. Utilitarians can justifiably disclaim the total variety. Let us herewith drop all reference to total strict liability.

But what of specific strict liability? Remember that this sort obtains when offenders against some laws, but not all, are strictly liable. Hence, if enacting a single strict liability law, in a single place, in any single period of time, would slightly increase utility, by comparison with alternatives, then utilitarians should regard strict liability as morally permissible.

Consider a law holding offenders strictly liable to the sanction of imprisonment for selling adulterated food, e.g., diseased or poisonous meat.[4] The harm caused by selling such food—pain, illness, death—is evident. Yet it is often extremely difficult to prove that a merchant sold such food voluntarily or through neglignece. But suppose a vendor, tempted to such sale, knew that, if caught, he would be strictly liable. In that case he could not hope to get off on some simulated excuse. Given this certitude of conviction, then, as H. L. A. Hart emphasizes, the deterrence threat of punishment is more effective.[5] Hence, we may expect that some of those tempted to commit the crime intentionally would not succumb. We may also expect a decline in undectectable negligence, since merchants would take extra precautions to avoid selling adulterated food. They know that once convicted, then, blameless or not, they go to jail.

Note that a similar utilitarian claim may be offered for a law prescribing vicarious punishment of parents for their children's offenses, e.g., illegal possession of heroin. Parental negligence is often difficult to ascertain. However, given such vicarious liability, at least some parents would expend extra effort to keep their children away from heroin.

A utilitarian rationale for strict liability may be summed up as follows: the denial of excuses toughens the deterrent threat of punishment. Hence, some of those who aspire to crime and recklessness, or those who would otherwise be undetectably negligent, will be effectively deterred from such misconduct. By reducing such doings, strict liability may, by comparison with other alternatives, best serve utility. I shall refer to this utilitarian argument for strict liability as *deterrence*.

Strict liability may, of course, have disutile effects. Consider that the ordinary citizen is deterred by the disgrace of imprisonment. However, this deterrent effect would decline if a practice is made of imprisoning morally innocent persons.

True enough. But there is no reason to think that any single such law would so weaken the threat of punishment as to be precluded by utilitarian standards.

Richard Brandt claims that the insecurity created by strict liability renders it valueless. "Imagine the pleasure of driving an automobile if one knew one could be *executed* for running down a child whom it was absolutely impossible to avoid striking."[6] But Brandt's claim, if true, only shows that a single kind of strict liability law (one making offenders liable to execution for involuntary motor homicide) should be unacceptable to utilitarians. He does not disprove what I take to be a virtual certainty: there is at least one occasion where the positive benefits of at least one strict liability law would be decisive utility-wise. Hence, specific strict liability should be acceptable to utilitarians.

Are we ready for retributivism? Not quite. H. L. A. Hart suggests that philosophers of punishment might do well to resist the traditional retributivist-utilitarian dichotomy. Let us respect Hart's wishes and consider first his view of strict liability apart from traditional classifications.

Hart believes that a system of legal excuses "maximizes individual freedom within the coercive framework of law." Why?

> First, the individual has an option between obeying or paying . . . Secondly, this system not only enables individuals to exercise this choice but increases the power of individuals to identify beforehand periods when the law's punishments will not interfere with them and plan their lives accordingly . . .
>
> . . . Where punishment is not so restricted, individuals will be liable to have their plans frustrated by punishments for what they do unintentionally, in ignorance, by accident or mistake . . .[7]

Thus, as Hart sees the matter, allowing legal excuses augments freedom of choice for potential involuntary offenders. I suggest, however, that his view is one-sided. According to *deterrence*, the denial of legal excuses would, in some instances, reduce crime. Hart would no doubt agree, for he emphasizes the deterrent value of strict liability in his critique of Bentham.

But Hart fails to note that the crime reduction consequent upon denying excuses would expand freedom of choice for those who might otherwise suffer from crime. Do not criminals interfere in their victim's lives, frustrating their plans? Do not criminals, by such interference, reduce their victims' capacity to effectively plan their future? Do not criminals thereby restrict their victims' capacity to effectively plan their future? Do not criminals thereby restrict their victims' effective exercise of free choice? Of course they do. In that case, the free choice consideration works both for and against legal excuses. As Hart claims, legal excuses enhance free choice for those who would not intentionally commit a crime. Their plans are not inhibited by the spectre of punishment for offenses committed unintentionally. But strict liability, in its way, also augments freedom of choice. By reducing crime, the denial of excuses increases such freedom for potential crime victims. They will not have their plans dashed by criminal interference. Hence, those who opt for legal excuses, as well as those who stand up for strict liability, may claim Hart's standard: more free choice.

I conclude that Hart's free choice argument against strict liability is not decisive.

Retributivism

Let us imagine ourselves as members of a legislative assembly. We have before us a proposal to amend the penal provisions of an existing law so that offenders against this law would be strictly liable to the sanction of imprisonment. We shall assume that no alternative to enacting the amendment has higher utility. If the law is so amended, it is virtually certain that a class of faultless offenders, to be called O's, would be punished. It is equally certain that then, and only then, would the effects stated in *deterrence* ensue. Crime, recklessness and negligence would decline. Thus potential victims of such misconduct, to be called H's, would be spared harm. Both O's and H's are decent people. A final detail: the possibility that any O is identical with any H is so unlikely that we may dismiss it from consideration.

This recital of data — with one exception — includes all the morally relevant facts of the case. Note that we know only in a general fashion that some punishment of O's would prevent some harm to H's. But how much punishment? How much harm? This we do not know yet, but we expect to be so informed.

An uncompromising retributivist would claim, however, that we know enough already to decide the case. Under no circumstances should O's be punished. Why not? Consider the following argument,

R: 1. No one ought ever to be wronged as a means of preventing foreseen harm to others.

2. Undeserved punishment always wrongs the person so punished.

Therefore:

3. No one ought ever to be punished undeservedly as a means of preventing foreseen harm to others.

Our retributivist would claim that premises (1) and (2) are both true. Hence, since R is valid, conclusion (3) is true. I shall claim, however, that although (1) may be true, (2) is in fact false. Undeserved punishment does not always wrong the person so punished. And if (2) is false, R does not prove (3) is true. Secondly, I shall claim that (3) is in fact false. Under some circumstances (to be specified), O's ought to be punished undeservedly for the sake of preventing harm to H's.

Let us consider the premises of R:
1. No one ought ever to be wronged as a means of preventing foreseen harm to others.

Why have some philosophers claimed (1)? Their claim is most plausibly put forth by showing that contravention of (1) violates a comparative principle which ranks moral obligations in order of priority. Such a comparative principle is expressed in the claim that the duty of non-maleficence is prior to the duty of beneficence or assistance. For example, a doctor has no right to murder X in order to keep Y alive. Wronging some as a means of preventing foreseen harm to others reverses the proper order of moral priorities.[8]

By so acting we also violate the comparative principle of double effect. According to this principle, the obligation to not *intend* evil takes precedence over any obligation to prevent or refrain from contributing causally to merely *foreseen* evil. An evil is intended if it is either one's aim ("really determines the will") or is a means to one's aim.[9] The doctor who wrongs X (murders him) as a means of preventing foreseen harm to Y(s) intends evil for the sake of preventing evil. Thus he violates the obligation which should have first claim on him.

A Kantian would certainly reject (1). But he would not make a comparative principle. The point of a comparative principle is to resolve a conflict between incompatible duties. Two duties are incompatible, in a given circumstance, if in that circumstance we can fulfill one only by violating the other. But for Kant, all duties are perfectly compatible, enjoined by a single principle of humanity:

> Act so that you treat humanity whether in your own person or in that of another, always as an end and never as a means only.[10]

Note however that the principle of humanity prescribes both

(h_1) Never treat a person as a means only
and
(h_2) Always treat a person as an end in himself

The duty of (h_1) is always a constituent of a compound duty: (h_1) and (h_2). Whenever one treats a person as a means only (e.g.) lies or steals) one also fails to treat him as an end in himself. But the duty of (h_2) is not always a constituent of the compound duty (h_1 and h_2). We violate the simple duty of (h_2) whenever we fail to act "as far as we can to further the ends of others ... (e.g.) happiness." The simple duty of (h_2) is, in fact, the duty of assistance. But when one fails in that duty by failing to assist someone, as one ought, one is not thereby treating that person as a means only.

I suggest that the compound duty (h_1 and h_2) is incompatible with the simple duty (h_2). If our doctor refuses to murder A, he adheres to the compound duty (h_1 and h_2). But in so doing he violates the simple duty (h_2), for he refrains from assisting B to live. Thus the principle of humanity prescribes incompatible duties.

But surely the doctor who refuses to murder A acts in the spirit of Kantian justice. Let us preserve this spirit by conceiving the principle of humanity as a comparative principle implying that the compound duty (h_1 and h_2) is prior to the simple duty (h_2). However, (h_1 and h_2) implies (1) of the retributivist argument. Thus, by acting contrary to (1), we violate Kant's principle of humanity, so conceived.

Each of the three comparative principles stated above implies (1). Let us assume that at least one of these comparative principles is true. In that case we may also assume that (1) is true as well.

Consider now premise (2) of R.

2. Undeserved punishment always wrongs the person punished.

I shall argue that (2) is false. In some circumstances, the imposition of undeserved legal punishment in order to avert harm to others does not wrong the person so punished. Here is why: suppose that A is required by law to sacrifice so that B not be harmed. I shall refer to these cases as imposed sacrifices. Would A be wronged in any such cases? No, he would not. Such imposition would suffice to wrong A if A had no moral duty to so assist B.

Let us distinguish clear cases where A has such a moral duty to B from those where he does not.

Assume the following: First, A has no relation to B which founds a special assistance obligation, e.g., doctor to patient. Second, B is a decent person and the moral quality of his distress is not bad, e.g., B is not afflicted with envy. Third, A's sacrifice is not itself immoral, e.g., he would not be betraying a trust for B's sake.

A clearly has no duty of sacrifice to members of a B group in cases of this sort:

> I. A's sacrifice would be most extreme. E.g., A has no duty to prevent the death or torture of members of a B group by volunteering for the same fate.
>
> II. Any B member's need for the benefit he would derive from A's sacrifice is less or slightly more than A's need for what A would sacrifice. E.g., each of the 3 members of a B group is suffering slightly more than A. A has 3 pain killing capsules. For A, 3 capsules would be totally effective, but less would be totally ineffective. But for each B member one capsule would be completely effective. A, however, has no duty to give his 3 capsules to the B members.

Suppose that A voluntarily made a I or II type sacrifice. In that case he would be doing much more than duty requires. Such an oversubscription to moral duty is a supererogatory performance, "an act ... which it would be good to do and neither good nor bad not to do."[10] Should such sacrifice be legally required of A he would indeed be wronged.

Thus, I suggest that in any imposed sacrifice, A is wronged if his sacrifice is such that, had he made it voluntarily, his performance would have been supererogatory. If A has no duty of sacrifice in a given circumstance, then A is clearly wronged in being required to so sacrifice.

Let us now look at situations where A clearly has a duty of sacrifice to members of a B group. A clearly has a duty of sacrifice in cases which are neither I or II type but where III obtains:

> III. There is a very great gap between the distress A would suffer because of his sacrifice and the greater degree of distress B would be spared thereby.

The following are III cases:

A discovers himself to be a carrier of some highly contagious and potentially fatal disease. It is virtually certain that he will communicate the disease to some B members around him. A has a duty to give himself up for quarantine — even with the grim prospect that such quarantine would very probably be permanent.

An A and B group are unjustly imprisoned by a military occupation. The A group is given a fairly adequate amount of food while the B group receives starvation rations. Members of A have a duty to give some of their food to the B group as long as they are both imprisoned.

A members have an effective and harmless pain killing drug which they use to alleviate an occasional bad headache. The A members should give the drug to B members who are suffering protracted physical agony and have no other way to relieve their pain.

Well-to-do A members ought to make a moderate financial sacrifice so that B members will not suffer freezing cold, disease or starvation. A members have this duty even if they are never made morally uncomfortable by seeing some B members.

A might object by saying, "But the money (or the drug) is *mine*." And so it is, legally speaking. But legal ownership does not always settle the question of moral entitlement. Consider the owner of an expensive fire extinguisher who, confronted with a burning child, insists, "But it's my fire extinguisher."

Are governments always obligated to impose type III sacrifices? Certainly not, if such an imposition would lead to disastrous results, as it might if members of Group A were principled egoists powerful enough to create havoc rather than tolerate inroads on their purses and principles. However, if the case is type III, and there are no other morally relevant facts to the contrary, then a government ought to impose the sacrifice on A members. They would not be wronged thereby.

Let us return to our retributivist argument, R:

1. No one ought ever to be wronged as a means to the end of preventing foreseen harm to others.
2. Undeserved punishment always wrongs the person punished.

Therefore:

3. No one ought ever to be punished undeservedly as a means of preventing foreseen harm to others.

But where imposing undeserved punishment turns out to be a type III sacrifice, then O's (the faultless offenders) are not wronged thereby. In that case (2) is false. Hence R, although valid, does not prove that (3) is true. Moreover, if O's undeserved punishment is a type III sacrifice, and there are no morally relevant facts to the contrary, then such punishment ought to be imposed on O's. Our hypothesis excludes any such morally relevant facts. Hence, if punishing O's undeservedly is indeed a type III sacrifice, O's should be so punished.

How would the utilitarian position on strict liability differ from the view I have taken here? A consistent utilitarian would endorse O's punishment if (given no other morally relevant facts) O's punitive suffering were envisaged as merely slightly less than H's (the potential victims) prevented pain. However, such an imposition on O's for the sake of H's is not a type III case, hence not allowed according to my view. (The case would be type III if and only if O's distress were *very much* less than H's.) If the utilitarian position were correct, then one ought to sacrifice for another's sake when (given no other morally relevant facts) the pain of one's sacrifice is only slightly less than the beneficiary's prevented pain. Such a sacrifice, when made voluntarily, is, however, an act of supererogation over and above what duty requires. Since we have no duty to so sacrifice voluntarily, then (given no other morally relevant facts) such sacrifice ought not be imposed on us.

Conclusions

It may be objected that I have neglected a morally relevant fact of our case. O's will not merely endure some degree of distress. They will be punished for an offense of which they are blameless. Their punishment is *undeserved*, a matter of some moral importance. This is perfectly true. But remember that, unless the amendment mentioned above passes (making offenders of the amended law strictly liable to imprisonment) and O's are punished, then H's will be victimized by crime or negligence. If our case is indeed type III, then the fate of H's would be very much worse than O's. But H's are good people. They do not deserve such a fate. Since neither O's nor H's deserve their respective envisaged ordeals, the desert of either cannot decide the case.

But, it may be objected, the notion of H's not deserving to suffer is surely odd. Such desert claims are normally made in contexts where individuals are conceived as offenders against the penal rule of some authority. The point of such a claim is to determine whether or not they deserve to suffer a penalty. O's are conceived as such persons, but H's are not. According to the objection, the insistence that these good

H's do not deserve their ordeal is to employ an abstractly moral and useless notion of desert. One might just as well assert that a person didn't deserve his last illness.

On the contrary, the assessment of penal desert requires just this abstractly moral notion of desert. To determine whether a proposed penalty is deserved, a lawmaker must assess that penalty in light of the gravity of the moral offense. What a person deserves to suffer is determined by the moral badness of his action, no matter what the law says. If a petty thief deserves to suffer his legal penalty, then a sadistic child beater deserves to suffer more, even if childbeating were perfectly legal. No one deserves to suffer for anything he does just because a law says so. If he did, then lawmakers would have no standard by which to make up deserved penalties for new offenses. To set such penalties, our abstract moral notion of desert is indispensable. Thus we are perfectly entitled to say H's have done no bad acts; hence they do not deserve to suffer at all.

I have assumed that the punishment envisaged for O's might turn out to be a type III imposed sacrifice. If O's sacrifice were type III, then the pain which H's are spared would be far worse than O's punitive distress. But it may be objected that this assumption is false. According to this objection, punitive pain is qualitatively worse than other sorts of misery. Punishment — even of one known as blameless — is humiliating. The ignominy of punishment belongs to a different continuum, incomparably worse than other varieties of pain. Hence, punishment can never truly be imposed as a type III sacrifice.

But is this true? Consider that an H's suffering as a victim of crime or negligence might turn out to be dreadful indeed. He might be assaulted, robbed of all he owns, maimed or disfigured, suffer protracted physical agony, even death. It is surely false that any such ordeal cannot be far worse than a prison sentence of six months to a year. Remember that we endorsed imposing the sacrifice of permanent quarantine on a disease carrier for the benefit of susceptible potential victims. Would not the ordeal of permanent quarantine be a more stringent sacrifice than six months to a year's imprisonment — humiliating or not?

Those who insist, however, that punitive suffering is incomparably worse than other kinds of distress should, if consistent, give up in large measure their right to punish anyone, guilty or innocent. Here is why: Consider now, not the blameless offender, but a full-fledged criminal, one who has intentionally committed a crime. How is justified punishment of such a person determined? Retributivists look backward, matching punitive pain to the moral gravity of the offense. Like for Like sets the limit which deserved punishment cannot exceed. But, given any plausible reading of Like for Like, how many offenders would deserve an ordeal which, *ex hypothesi*, is incomparably worse than other sorts of suffering?

The utilitarian punisher looks forward, measuring the hurt of punishment against the predictable suffering of predictable crime. The hurt of punishment must not be worse than the hurt it presumably prevents. Thus, for utilitarians, the standard of Like *before* Like sets the upper limit which justified punishment must not transgress. But if, *ex hypothesi*, punishment is incomparably worse than the misery it averts, the utilitarians lose the right to punish the guilty as well as the innocent.

Thus, those who insist that the pain of punishment belongs to a *different and worse* continuum of pain should, if consistent, give up, either in large measure or completely, the right to punish the guilty.

Finally, it may be objected that my hypothesis is itself quite unrealistic. For example, it is surely very unlikely that we could, as I have hypothesized, be virtually certain that, unless the amendment passes and O's are imprisoned for a specified period, H's will undergo some specified degree of suffering. We might know very well that a carrier will communicate his disease. Hence we impose permanent quarantine on him. But it is hardly probable that we could have such certainty in our punishment case.

Yes, our punishment case is quite unlikely, deliberately so. It is one thing to reject undeserved punishment because the benefits are uncertain. It is quite another to reject it because it is undeserved punishment. By considering the unlikely case — where the benefits are certain — we can be all the clearer when we get down to real cases.

NOTES

[1] "Strict Liability in the Criminal Law," Richard Wasserstrom, reprinted from the *Stanford Law Review XII*, 1960 in *Freedom and Responsibility*, ed. Herbert Morris. (emphasis added.)

[2] I suspect that many defendants in so-called strict liability convictions, are in fact, presumed by their judge or jury to be negligent. *Lindberg* is instructive in this regard. Lindberg, a bank officer acting on erroneous information concerning a loan he made, violated statutory regulations governing such loans. He was convicted of a felony. The Supreme Court of Washington in turning down Lindberg's appeal claimed that correct information about the loan was "a matter of record to which he (Lindberg) had access . . . To fail to note it is *negligence*." The court therefore denied that Lindberg was

in fact "innocent of wrong." *The Pacific Reporter* Vol. 215 p. 44, 1923 (emphasis added).

Freund claims that in public welfare cases (where strict liability convictions have been most frequent) ignorance of fact "implies a fault, and it must be assumed that with due diligence the true character of the act could have been ascertained." In that case, what is assumed is negligence. Defendants presumably should have but didn't take reasonable care to ascertain the facts. (*Ibid.* p. 45).

³Jeremy Bentham, *Principles of Morals and legislation*, Ch. XIII.

⁴Imprisonment for such an offense was in fact upheld in *Hobbs* v. *Winchester Corp. 1910.* "It has been held in Hobbs v. Winchester Corp. that a butcher who innocently and without negligence sold diseased meat violated the statute, and that the provision for imprisonment as one of the sanctions did not alter the irrelevance of *mens rea.*" J. Hall, *General Principles of Criminal Law*, Ch. X, *App.*

⁵H. L. A. Hart, "*Prolegomenon to the Principles of Punishment,*" in *Punishment and Responsibility*, Oxford Paperback pp. 18-20.

⁶Richard Brandt, *Ethical Theory*, p. 493 (emphasis added).

⁷H. L. A. Hart, *Ibid.*, p. 23.

⁸"It seems clear to me that non-maleficence (not injuring others) is apprehended as a duty distinct from that of beneficience, and as a duty of a more stringent character . . . the duty of non-maleficence is . . . *prima facie* more binding. We should not in general consider it justifiable to kill one person in order to keep another alive, or to steal from one in order to give alms to another." David Ross, *The Right and the Good*, pp. 22, 23 Oxford, 1965.

"To refrain from inflicting injury ourselves is a stricter duty than to prevent other people from inflicting injury . . . We are not forced to the conclusion that the size of the evil must always be our guide." Philippa Foot, "The Problem of Abortion and the Doctrine of the Double Effect," *Oxford Review*, No. 5 (1967) reprinted in *Moral Problems*, ed. James Rachels, Harper & Row, 1971 paperback.

⁹Thomas J. O'Donnell, *Morals in Medicine*, pp. 41-44, S. J. Newman Press, Maryland, 1956.

¹⁰Immanuel Kant, *Foundations of the Metaphysics of Morals*, LLA edition, p. 47.

H. J. McCLOSKEY
The Morality of Punishment of the "Moral" Criminal

In this paper I am concerned with the justification, if any, of punishment of those who break the law or who engage in grievous wrongdoing because they believe that they are morally bound so to act. The kinds of criminals whose punishment I shall discuss include patriotic and dutiful "war criminals," conscientious objectors, civil disobedients, political offenders in general, those guilty of crimes under laws relating to industrial conditions and disputes, and many of those who are punished for "comtempt of court" and related offenses. Much has been written since the Second World War concerning the punishment of "war criminals," and much has been written, especially during the past decade, concerning the rights of individuals to be conscientious objectors, civil disobedients, political offenders, and the like; but in recent times much less has been written concerning the right to become a criminal under industrial laws, or to commit acts condemned as "contempt of court." More important, the other side of the problem, that of the right of the state to punish those who disobey the law on moral grounds, has either been ignored or dealt with in a very perfunctory way. For example, many who have argued for the right of individuals to be civilly disobedient have confined their accounts within the context of constitutional, liberal, democratic states, and have simply and uncritically assumed that such states have the right to punish. They have suggested further that unless the civil disobedients concerned accept and submit to the punishment, they are revolutionaries, not civil disobedients; for acceptance of punishment is seen as being essential as a condition for showing respect for the legal and political system as a whole. Others have seen that states other than constitutional, liberal democracies may have and exercise legitimate authority, and that civil disobedience may be justified in such states, but again the same assumption is made that the civil disobedient, to be such and not a revolutionary, must accept the punishment due to his offense, the underlying assumption remaining that the state has not simply the legal but also the moral right to administer such punishment. Such discussions impress me as being crude and oversimplified. It is true that they avoid the common error that has almost become dogma today, that rights and duties are correlative in the sense that the right to disobey as a civil disobedient implies the existence of a duty in the state not to impose or to seek to impose punishments on such offenders. On the other hand, the case for such punishments, their moral justification where they are justified — and it would seem that they may also be justified in states other than constitutional, liberal, democracies — needs to be established. This is both important and necessary since the more widely accepted accounts of the morality of punishment fail to provide plausible, morally acceptable grounds of justification for the punishment of "moral" criminals, including those who seemingly ought to be punished.

The traditional accounts of punishment by and within states which are currently treated as being of major importance are the utilitarian, the retributive, and the compromise, combined utilitarian-retributive theories. These may be explained briefly as follows: The utilitarian account of punishment maintains that to be justified, punishment must be useful, useful by way of promoting pleasure, happiness, or goods, or by way of lessening pain, unhappiness, or evils. The act utilitarian insists that to be morally justified, the individual punishment must be useful; the rule utilitarian, on the other hand, insists only on the institution of punishment as a whole being useful. Here I do not wish to develop the problems and objections urged against the utilitarian theory which are that punishment of potential criminals, of those not responsible for their actions, and of innocent persons believed to be quilty, may be useful and that such systems and institutions of punishment as allow such punishments may also be useful, and hence have utilitarian justifications. For the purpose of this paper, it is sufficient to note that the utilitarian sees punishment as justified if useful, in the specific instance or as part of a useful institution, and that it may be useful in preventing a criminal repeating a crime by way of preventive detention, mutilation, execution, or by reforming him, and by way of deterring the criminal and other potential criminals.

The retributive theory of punishment, on the other hand, makes desert crucial, if the punishment that is administered is to be morally just punishment. To be *prima facie* justified, punishment must be deserved. For it to be deserved, the one punished must be responsible for an offense, and the punishment must be commensurate with the offense. Punishment which is not for an offense, or which exceeds what is commensurate with the offense, is unjust. Punishment which is less than is deserved needs special justification in terms of other moral considerations, such as harm to innocent persons, other considerations of mercy, or concern for values the realization of which would be jeopardized by such punishment. The compromise combined utilitarian-retributive theory, which is often canvassed but generally defended only by way of a critique of utilitarian theories of punishment, maintains that only the guilty can properly be punished, where the guilty person is one who is responsible for his actions, and the punishment is determined firstly by what is commensurate with the offense and then modified on the basis of utilitarian considerations if and only if they dictate less than is deserved. In terms of this third view, utilitarian considerations are seen as providing adequate grounds for awarding as just, punishment which is less than is commensurate with the offense.

Because of its brevity, this account is necessarily somewhat philosophically crude; but it does serve to highlight distinctive features of the three accounts. Many other accounts of justice and morality in punishment have been advanced, many as versions of the retributive theory, for example, that punishment is an expression of moral condemnation, that it is educative, that it is to be justified in terms of the protection of rights, that it must be imposed so as not to disappoint the reasonable expectations of the community, that punishment serves as an atonement, that it annuls the offense, that it ensures or seeks to ensure that the wicked do not prosper from their crimes; but the three theories of punishment outlined above are those that I regard as being the most important, and they seem generally so to be regarded today. The contention of this paper is that none of these three accounts does justice to what is just and to what is moral in the area of the punishment of "moral" criminals. It will be contended that a more complex account of the punishment of "moral" criminals is necessary, that desert is a basic consideration in all that is properly to be called punishment, but that considerations of desert may justifiably be overridden by the need for instruments of social control to safeguard and promote values including those that underlie the utilitarian and retributive theories of punishment — values such as pleasure, happiness and freedom from pain, justice, respect for persons, honesty, as well as goods such as true belief, knowledge, rationality, human self-development and the goods attainable and capable of being appreciated thereby. Some punishment necessary for such social control is better thought of not as punishment but as akin to penalties in games necessary for the existence and playing of the games; other necessary, desirable measures of social control commonly described as punishment, although not punitive in essence or intent, are more akin to internment in war, quarantining to prevent epidemics, treatment to "cure" the involuntary social misfit, etc.

War Crimes and War Criminals

Here I wish to consider war criminals at two levels. The first is the level of rulers who issue directives to subordinates to engage in immoral acts in wartime, who by virtue of their orders are declared to be "war criminals" whether or not they believe to be right and obligatory what they direct their subordinates to do. Second are those moral agents at the subordinate level, the soldier, research scientist, worker, citizen, who are given orders to act in immoral ways and who obey those orders.

Consider those "war criminals," the rulers. In this century at least there has been a strong, widely-held belief that rulers who instigate war crimes of the kinds perpetrated by the Nazis —mass killings of Jews, unjust deterrent punishments of innocents as at Lidice, and the like — ought to be punished. Various attempts have been made to justify such punishments. The defenders of this position point out that there has been an entering into treaties and agreements which outlaw such actions. However, not all offending nations have entered into such agreements; and, of those that have, not all have done so freely. Further, there is the problem of the continuing identity of the nation which entered into the agreement some 20, 30, or 50 years ago — can it reasonably be identified as the same nation which committed the offenses for which punishment is sought. Complex issues also arise in respect of appeals to international law. It might, for instance, be asked: "What authority do international law and the courts which interpret and apply it and the agencies which enforce it have for those who do not recognize as law what is claimed by others to be international law?" "What claim to be interpretative, adjudicative, and enforcement authorities, have those who claim to be such?" Parallels, some possessed of some plausibility and some totally without plausibility, may be drawn between elements of international law repudiated by states and both common and statute law repudiated by citizens of a state. In a desperate move in their attempt to justify punishment which they believe ought to be inflicted, some speak of the case for introducing retroactive legislation, seemingly by some very indeterminate body with few claims to real authority, to render illegal, conduct which at the time at which it occurred was legal. Such retroactive legislation seeks to make illegal and criminal what, in its absence, is simply conduct believed by the exponents of the retroactive legislation to be gravely immoral. The position is complicated by the fact that the immoralities which those eager to inflict punishment claim to be crimes are commonly seen by the alleged criminals to be the very opposite of immoralities, and to be instead the fulfillment of duty. Eichmann so argued in respect of his alleged "war crimes." He may well have been insincere in this, but not all rulers who are alleged to be "war criminals" are insincere when they make such claims. Hence arises the problem as to whether there is justification for the punishment which is so commonly believed to be both desirable and merited for crimes committed by rulers who do or instigate what they believe they ought to do or instigate.

Before considering the case for punishing dutiful rulers who perpetrate what we deem to be grave immoralities, it is desirable that we consider the various lesser "war criminals," the subordinates. Here we may distinguish a number of different kinds of cases. Firstly, there is the person acting on the orders of a superior authority who does wrong, believing it to be right. An example would be that of the dutiful Nazi concentration camp commandant who exterminates his prisoners as ordered, believing that he is acting rightly both in obeying orders and in killing the prisoners. Secondly, there is the person who does what is objectively wrong, but who does not reflect on the rightness or wrongness of what he does because he sees his overriding duty as that of obeying the orders of his recognized (or recognized as legitimate) authority. Thirdly, there is the individual who does what he believes to be morally gravely wrong in obedience to the orders of a legitimate superior authority in a war directed at safeguarding values and standards which he believes to be true values and standards; for example, he kills innocent women and children as a deterrent against fifth column activity by adult males. He believes this to be morally wrong even though it may be necessary to shorten the war and to bring victory. Fourthly, there is the person who does what he believes to be wrong in obedience to a superior authority which he repudiates on moral grounds but obeys from prudence; for example, a morally enlightened German medical researcher who experiments in a deadly way on human specimens. Fifthly, there is the person who chooses to become a criminal in his own country (it could be a constitutional democracy devoted to fostering racialist discrimination), by disobeying the lawful orders of a legitimate superior authority who commands what is morally evil or what is believed to be morally evil by him who renders himself a criminal by his disobedience. Among these subordinates are some who have freely chosen their roles and duties, and others who have been conscripted or otherwise coerced into them. Many of the former, in adopting their roles and duties, know they may be involved in what some, many, or even they themselves believe to be immoral. The moral positions in respect of punishment of these various groups are therefore significantly different. Whether or not the state is a constitutional democracy *may* also bear on the issue of the right to punish.

What then is the justification of punishments that are commonly recommended in such cases? Is punishment of such rulers and subordinates ever justified? When and to what extent, if any, is it relevant whether the state is a constitutional, democratic state, or an authoritarian one which is accepted as legitimate, or one whose rulers have seized power by unconstitutional use of force?

Among the essential features of the retributive theory that punishment, to be just, must be deserved are that the punishment must be administered by a proper authority (as distinct from a mere power) to an offender for an offense, which he knew or could have come to have known to be such, where the offender is responsible for his action and where the penalty or range of penalties is known or knowable before the offense and is known to be commensurate with the offense. Mitigating, extenuating circumstances are of course relevant here.

Where there is an acceptance by the rulers of international law and of an authority to enforce it, a case can be made for retributive punishment for offenses against it according to desert. Where the existence or "legality" of international law and/or of an authority to administer it is denied, the case for punishment is more difficult to establish in terms of the retributive theory. Where there has been a breach of an agreement by the alleged immoral ruler, what would seem to be fitting would be the imposition of penalties and the insistence on reparation of the kinds that hold for certain breaches of contract, rather than the infliction of retributive punishment. Agreements and contracts may specify the penalties to be imposed for the breach of them. With rulers who do or instigate what they believe to be right and obligatory, but which is deemed by those who seek to punish them to be morally gravely wrong, where the rulers have repudiated international law as not law, and either not entered into an agreement to refrain from such conduct or have unfreely entered into such an agreement, or whose predecessors have done so unwillingly, or at such a remote times as to involve difficulties concerning the moral identity of the past and present state, there is first the obvious difficulty concerning who or what possesses the authority to punish, and, there is also the problem of the lack of proper promulgation and knowability of the offense. To punish a ruler for what may be a false belief, when he has applied himself conscientiously to reflecting about what is right or wrong, is to make what morally cannot rightly be made to be a punishable offense to be such. It is temptingly easy to claim, but often impossible to substantiate, that the conscientious, dutiful war criminal is really insincere in his claims. It is true that some who claim to have acted from duty are insincere, but many others appear to be completely sincere. In any case, the problem concerning the right of any state or group of persons backed by force to punish the rulers of another state as criminals remains a very real one for the retributivist, whether or not the rulers be rulers of a constitutional democracy, an accepted, legitimate, authoritarian regime, or a state from which the legitimate rulers have been ousted and destroyed. The problem would be eliminated by general acceptance of a detailed code of international law with procedures for changes in the law and for location of the authority to interpret and enforce the laws and formal procedures to renew acceptance or to opt out. Meanwhile, there remains a real problem for the retributivist, yet it is he with his concern that the criminal receive his deserts who is often most deeply committed to the punishing of such rulers.

The "immoral" but strictly speaking non-criminal conduct of subordinates raises similar difficulties for the retributivist. If there were a God to enforce moral law, and the moral law were knowable to all who sought to know it, there would be a case for divine punishment of rulers and subordinates alike who failed to do what morally they ought to do and what they knew or could know that they morally ought to do. However, here we are concerned with the justification of the punishment of some men by other men for moral offenses which were not criminal offenses under the laws of the states in which the moral offenders live. In our first example, the "criminal" does what he sincerely believes to be morally and legally right. In the second, he attends more specifically to the legality of his action, seeing its legality as basic to its morality. In the third example, he sees the act as legal but immoral, immoral not in respect of the ends to be achieved, but by virtue of the nature of the means. To punish the former two persons as "war criminals" is to punish those who have acted in strict accord with the law, doing what they sincerely believe to be right. Hence, it would be for a non-authority, the victors (in a war or civil war), to take it on themselves to make it *a crime* to hold, and act on the basis of, false belief. In the third case, the person believed to be wrong what his subsequent judges deemed to be wrong, but he opted to obey the law and hence not to be a criminal in the usual sense of "criminal." The main obstacle to any attempt to justify punishing him is the absence of a competent authority to enforce as law what is not law but simply the morality of the judges of the victorious party. What is both relevant and significant here is that even in a society such as Australia, in which there is an accepted constitutionally instituted authority, we deny the state the right to render a crime, and to punish as such, any act of gross immorality which it has not previously rendered by law a punishable crime. (The acceptance and modes of interpretation of common law, especially in Great Britain, render this contention in need of qualification in respect of detail but not of substance — the case of *Shaw versus the Director of Public Prosecutions* is relevant here.*) How much more difficult, then, is it to justify punishing those who act legally but knowingly (and even more so those who act unknowingly) immorally? Who or what has the authority to determine what is right

---

*Shaw v. Director of Public Prosecution (1962) 2 A.E.R. An easily accessible account of this case can be found in R. Wasserstrom (ed.) *Morality and the Law* (Belmont, Calif., Wadsworth Publishing Company, Inc., 1971), pp. 127-131.

and wrong so as to be entitled, in the absence of a law enforcing his moral view and empowering him to inflict punishment and in the presence of a law to the contrary, to render action contrary to his belief "criminal" and "punishable" in some significant senses? Thus all three examples raise for the retributivist the problems of the location and justification of the authority to punish and of the justification of the authority to promulgate or determine which immoralities *qua* immoralities are crimes simply because they are or are believed to be gross immoralities. The former two examples encounter the problem that they involve treating unavoidable moral ignorance or error as a moral fault, a problem which presupposes an objectivist ethical position, whereas the latter typically goes hand in hand with the contentions that "Ought implies can" and "Can implies can know." The fifth case is that of the seemingly justified punishment by the state of him who on moral grounds rejects the directives of the state and thereby renders himself strictly speaking a criminal, a "war" criminal if he is a soldier who disobeys a directive in war to slaughter innocent women and children. The punishment of such a person raises the problem of the justification of punishment of conscientious objectors. The example is more interesting, and raises a more serious problem, where the directive emanates from a ruler in a constitutional, liberal, democratic society. In the case of the person described in the fourth example, we may be less inclined to object to the imposition of punishment, yet the philosophical justification of such punishment remains a difficult problem for the retributivist.

The problems posed for the utilitarian by such cases are significantly different. For the utilitarian, it is the utility, not simply of the punishment but of the whole enterprise of administering punishment for such unpromulgated offenses by non-, pseudo-, and quasi-authorities. In the case of the rule utilitarian there are the added problems concerning the utility of *treating as if it is institutionalized punishment with known rules and knowable penalties, applied using fair, useful procedures for determining guilt or innocence, the kinds of arrangements such punishments would in fact involve.* Punishment under common law offenses is less institutionalized than rule utilitarianism depicts justified rule utilitarian punishment as being. Punishment where there are no rules declaring the action a crime, or where the rules declare non-performance of the act a crime, is even further removed from the rule utilitarian's model of institutionalized punishment. For the utilitarian, it is the utility of the punishment as part of the enterprise of punishment that is decisive. Whether or not punishment, for him, can properly be administered by persons who are not accepted as legitimate authorities, depends on this. There are very good utilitarian reasons for caution here. The question of such punishment of war criminals usually arises in situations in which there are ample alternative ways of preventing the "criminal" from repeating his offenses other than by preventive detention, mutilation, execution, or reform of his moral, non-utilitarian character or his utilitarian calculating ability. (He is usually unlikely so to be placed as to be able to commit or commission similar crimes in the future.) Hence deterrence of others must provide the main utilitarian ground for favoring such punishment. Yet it seems highly unlikely that future, ambitious rulers of new, powerful states will be deterred by such punishment having been inflicted on past rulers who were defeated in wars which they entered in the expectation that they would win. At best it might make them more cautious about embarking upon wars until fully prepared and reasonably confident of success. Similarly, given the widely accepted utilitarian argument in favor of punishment for crimes against criminal laws based on the deterrent effect of such punishment, it would seem unlikely that subordinates and ordinary citizens generally would be moved to risk punishment by their own state as a result of breaking immoral laws from *fear of deterrent punishment which might be administered by some quasi-authority which might emerge, and which might punish them if their rulers were to be defeated.* In brief, it cannot seriously be contended that the punishment of minor Nazi war criminals, those who from duty or prudence or habitual obedience carried out immoral, legal orders, would provide a serious deterrent which surpasses the deterrent provided by punishment by their rulers for breaches of their laws, where their laws enjoin immoral acts. Nonetheless, it is true that such punishment has the effect of seriously raising doubts about the truth or validity of the standards on the basis of which the so-called criminals acted, and to this extent the punishment has an educative, deterrent effect. Because of the non-institutional, rule-less nature of an enterprise of punishment along these lines, most rule utilitarian arguments relating to the justification of that punishment which is claimed to have a rule utilitarian justification are either irrelevant or run counter to the demand that such punishment be administered, and this for reasons relating to the rule utilitarian's attempt to incorporate into rule utilitarianism what he believes to be true in the retributive theory.

Having said this, it remains true that the desire, indeed, the demand for punishment of war criminals persists, and impresses most of us as a reasonable demand. It goes hand in hand with a general belief that they ought to get what they deserve, namely, suffering and even death. Yet neither a thoughtful application of the retributive nor of the utilitarian approach to the morality of punishment seems to provide a foundation on which to build a justification of such punishment. Is there then nothing more to be said of the matter? I suggest that there is much more to be said. That the use of organized force under the general description of punishment of those deemed guilty of moral offenses which threaten basic human values — respect for persons, justice, honesty, happiness, pleasure and freedom from pain, and the various other goods acknowledged by various ideal utilitarians, true belief, knowledge, rationality, self-development, beauty and aesthetic excellence — may be justified becomes evident from reflection on these values and on what can be achieved by such use of organized force. Non-legal, illegal, quasi-legal, and legal non-punitive uses of force to maintain and realize such values may be similarly justified. The device of using organized force under the general description of punishment, inaccurate though the description may sometimes be, may often be justified in terms of the utility of the description by way of its effect of restricting and controlling such use of force to those guilty of offenses, albeit moral offenses, which threaten basic human values. Such punishment is educative and, in a very broad sense, deterrent because it is educative in respect of such non-utilitarian and utilitarian values. Such education concerning values would *ipso facto* be education relating to human rights.

Punishment of Conscientious Objector Criminals

Here I construe, perhaps with some degree of arbitrariness, a conscientious objector criminal as one who breaks the law in order to perform a serious duty, either by abstaining from doing what he believes to be positively evil (and what perhaps is positively evil), or by doing what he believes he positively ought to do as a stringent duty, where his concern is with his own moral integrity rather than with the influencing of others to act as he himself does. Thus a pacifist who is a trained civilian pilot who refuses to serve as a bomber pilot, or a Roman Catholic surgeon who refuses to obey a law which obliges him to perform an abortion to save a mother's life, or a doctor who, contrary to the law but from a belief that it is a serious duty incumbent on him, aborts a twelve year old girl who has been raped, might reasonably be regarded as conscientious objector criminals. By contrast, the civil disobedient is here construed as one who breaks the law from a sense of duty, not necessarily to avoid the neglect of a serious duty damaging to his/her moral integrity, but in order to encourage others to do likewise, to right a wrong by having the law changed. The law to be changed is either that which is infringed or some other law, where the former may be a just, fair, useful law, but such that the breach of it causes inconvenience or even hardship which attracts attention to and even support for the demand for reform or repeal of the offending law. Thus, according to my use of terms, a conscientious objector criminal may, but need not be a civil disobedient criminal, and many civil disobedient criminals will not be conscientious objector criminals.

The retributive theory of punishment is essentially a theory of moral punishment according to moral desert. It is not a theory concerning punishment on the basis of legal desert except and only in so far as legal desert can be explained in terms of moral desert. The notion of legal desert, when separated from that of moral desert, is an elusive one. An offense may be a serious legal offense but not a serious moral offense. This is so when a severe legal penalty is attached to the legal offense. Thus in the U.S.A. tax evasion is a serious legal offense with correspondingly serious legal desert; in Australia it is a relatively minor legal offense with correspondingly less legal desert. Morally, the offense would seem to be equally serious or equally minor in each country, apart from considerations of the side effects of punishments of evaders who are detected and punished with consequent harm to their dependants. More generally, it would seem possible for a person to be legally guilty and morally innocent, and legally innocent and morally guilty, with corresponding differences in respect of legal and moral desert. Although it is usual for exponents of the retributive theory to apply it to punishment by the state in respect of offenses against the law, its logical standing is as a theory of ideal moral punishment to be administered by the moral authority, and *by authorities in the state qua moral authorities, for offenses against the law in so far as political authorities are thought of as moral authorities, and the legal offenses as genuine moral offenses.* (This is no accident as early exponents of the retributive theory saw the state as having divine moral authority and viewed offenses against it as moral offenses against God.) Many legal offenses in themselves are not moral offenses and become such only by being made legal offenses — for example, bringing secretly into the country two and not simply the one radio permitted by the customs regulations. Other actions which constitute offenses against the law may in fact constitute legitimate and even morally obligatory exercises of a person's rights — for example, the offense of a parent in educating his own child well, he being well qualified to do so, contrary to the law which demands that he send his child to a school to which his child is zoned and which is staffed by incompetent teachers who yet seek to indoctrinate the children with false, racialist beliefs. It is also relevant whether the citizen has consented, conditionally or unconditionally, to obey the state in a significant sense of "consented," for such consent may give rise to conflicts of *prima facie* rights and duties for the state and citizen alike. These and other considerations make for the difficulty of simply and uncritically transposing the moral theory of retributive punishment to the whole arena of the state with its legal offenses which constitute crimes.

A situation in which some actions which constitute legal offenses and are also morally right and obligatory actions may arise under a law which in general is just and right, but unjust and wrong in some one or more of its particular applications. It may also arise because the law is an unjust law, unjust in most or all of its applications. This situation may arise where the law emanates from a just, legitimate authority, and equally, from a usurped, illegitimate, even illegal power, where the former and even the latter may or may not be a constitutional, liberal, democratic state. (Suppose there had been a temporarily successful English democratic revolution at the time of the French Revolution, which introduced "illegal," unjust property laws.)

The problems which confront the retributivist here are manifold. He needs to offer an account of punishment under laws which are unjust in general or in particular applications — as justified or as unjustified — in just, legitimate states, but he also has to explain the case for justifiable punishment in states where the legitimacy of the authority is questionable. (Clearly the crimes of murder and at least certain kinds of stealing, blackmail, and rape ought to be punished, and were rightly punished even in states such as Hitler's Germany, Stalin's U.S.S.R., and Franco's Spain.) The retributivist position and its problems are further complicated by the fact that the conscientious objector criminal may be seriously mistaken in his moral beliefs, as too may the political authority which lays down the laws and determines what constitutes a crime. Thus, to be a theory of justice in punishment which has practical relevance to actual societies, the retributive theory must at least provide guidelines, if not detailed answers, to what constitutes moral and just punishment in a variety of different kinds of societies, in which the laws may be just or unjust, in general or only in specific cases. The retributive theory must suggest answers for societies in which: (i) unjust laws are rightly believed by the criminal to be unjust; (ii) just laws are wrongly believed to be unjust; (iii) unjust laws are wrongly believed to be just; (iv) just laws are seen to be just in general but to be unjust in respect of particular applications in societies of different political structures and constitutions. It would be possible to approach these and related problems from three standpoints: that of the conscientious criminal, that of the sincere, morally concerned political authority, and that of the impartial, uninvolved observer. I shall seek to cover these various standpoints.

To punish an individual for an offense which he cannot/could not know to be an offense due to unavoidable ignorance is to deny him his deserts. (I have taken for granted in this paper that there can be sincere diversity and conflict concerning basic moral beliefs because the facts of anthropology when carefully analysed, and those known to us concerning beliefs in twentieth century societies, separately and jointly force this conclusion on the impartial thinker). To punish an individual for doing what he rightly believes to be right, whatever the state authorities may think, is again *prima facie* at least not to give him his deserts. If it is disobedience of a law in general that is involved, we may wish to argue that punishment is permissible or even desirable, depending on how basic the law is to the maintenance of the society and the nature and degree of its injustice; yet it is hard to formulate a satisfactory justification of such punishment in terms of the retributive theory. If it is in respect of particular applications of the law, for example, conscripting pacifists in a just war, or compelling Roman Catholic doctors to perform abortions to save women's lives if they are the only doctors available, the case for punishment is generally weaker than if the law is in general unjust; yet in both types of cases, it may on occasion, and depending on the relevant circumstances, reasonably be believed that punishment is desirable and even necessary. Since it is beliefs — the beliefs of the authorities and those of the citizens — on the basis of which the case for punishment arises and in terms of which it must be determined, and since the retributive theory ideally relates to real offenses and not to mere supposed offenses, the relevance of the theory is further complicated. It is fully relevant if we adopt the morally very questionable view that a man has done what he ought when he has done what he believes he ought to have done. On the basis of that position, the sincere, mistaken authority would be justified in imposing retributive punishment, and the sincere, conscientious criminal would be justified in breaking the law and seeking to evade the punishment as unjust, undeserved punishment. In fact, it would seem that the moral position that is most defensible here is that a man cannot be obliged to do what is objectively right if he cannot know that it is right, not that he has done what he ought in doing what he wrongly believes he ought to do. If this is so, the retributive theory is relevant only in so far as we can have or lay reasonable claim to true moral beliefs. However, it does entail that the state needs a special justification for punishing a person who commits a crime in order to do what he sincerely believes he ought to do.

Again, there are situations in which the authorities may believe, or even know, that the citizen is acting rightly in breaking the law; for example, where the law is one that is just in general and unjust and evil in certain particular applications. Just states seek, not always with success, to avoid or to remedy in part such evils. In such cases of the conscientious person committing a crime to avoid doing an injustice or evil, it would follow from the retributive theory that the individual not be punished. A simple example to illustrate this point would be that of the just traffic law which renders it illegal ever to cross double lines, and of the conscientious person who breaks the law by crossing the lines to avoid a head-on collision which would have resulted in injuries and deaths. Non-enforcement of the law by not prosecuting offenders is not always desirable in such cases.

Problems arise in this area also for the utilitarian account of punishment. The utilitarian is committed to reforming the dutiful, conscientious criminal, even the dutiful, conscientious, utilitarian criminal, if such reformation is likely to result in greater overall utility by way of obedience to the law in general. Much is made by utilitarian writers of the danger of anarchy and the evils thereof if individuals are permitted or even encouraged to use their own judgments about which laws are fit to obey, or about which laws are 'unjust' and unfit to obey. Past history, and a consideration of the many reforms that have resulted from conscientious disobedience without the occurrence of revolutions or anarchy in Western democracies, suggest that at best such arguments overestimate a danger and do not represent serious commentaries on the facts.

The utilitarian is also committed to preventing the dutiful, conscientious objector from repeating his crime if, overall, this involves less harm. Internment, quarantining, imprisonment, mutilation, execution are measures which, given the relevant circumstance, may properly be directed by utilitarian authorities against the dutiful man, even the dutiful utilitarian, if such measures are more useful, all things considered, than any other measures. Thus to treat the person who seeks to do his duty, or who does what is in fact his duty (and here we may consider both the case of the utilitarian and of the non-utilitarian), would appear to be an abandonment of the standpoint of morality and a treatment of moral agents as things to be manipulated rather than as autonomous moral beings possessed of the right and duty to make and act on the basis of their considered moral beliefs.

The main utilitarian argument for punishment of such individuals is based on the utility of deterring others. Even if the conscientious objector criminal is a sincere utilitarian who correctly determines his utilitarian duty in disobeying the law, it may be right and obligatory for the authorities to punish him because, if they do not do so, others may harmfully and wrongly imitate the "criminal," or he may repeat the same kind of crime in the future when it lacks the same utilitarian justification. That is to say, the utilitarian may have to subscribe to the paradox that the particular individual is right to act in a criminal way and that the state is right to punish him to stop him from wrongly repeating his crime and to deter others from imitating him when such imitation is unjustified. The following example illustrates this kind of issue. The law forbidding murder is, overall, a just and useful law. An exception to it, that of seeking secretly to murder the head of a drug-peddling organization dealing in heroin who has successfully eluded legal punishment, by having it appear that his death was due to an unavoidable motor accident is, or may be, for the utilitarian, a morally justified departure from the rule, whether or not the truth comes to be known. If it does come to be known, the crime may still have fulfilled the conscientious utilitarian's duty, although it would then probably be right for the utilarian rulers to seek to convict and punish him to prevent him from acting criminally in similar, yet relevantly dissimilar cases, and to deter others from murders which lack real utilitarian justifications.

In brief, my thesis is that the utilitarian approach to the punishment of the conscientious objector criminal — and there must be some such even in the ideal, practical utilitarian society — is morally unsatisfactory. A much more complex account of the morality of punishment is needed here. Again, while the retributive theory encounters difficulties, desert remains a *relevant* consideration in determining whether to punish, and, if there is to be punishment, how much should there be. Conscientiousness is relevant to desert. However, other considerations are also relevant to the punishment — not least its utility or harmfulness in respect of protecting, maintaining, realizing values such as those of respect for persons, justice, honesty, human happiness, pleasure, rationality, knowledge, self-development, aesthetic excellence. To respect the conscientious objector criminal is to respect a person, but it may be to do so at the expense of respect for many other persons, as well as at the expense of justice, happiness, and many other goods. Again, the justification of punishment, and its lack of justification when it is not justified in respect of the conscientious criminal, are to be found in terms of the values secured and recognized and those jeopardized, ignored, or lost. The conscientiousness of the criminal is one value, the justice or injustice of the law relates to another value — the kind of society and state from which the law emanates introduces other values and disvalues. If social control is necessary to realize and maintain the overriding values, and if punishment of the conscientious criminal is the only or, in terms of these values, the least harmful way of achieving the necessary social control, such punishment may be justified. However, into the calculus will go considerations of desert, respect for persons, justice, happiness, pleasure, and the like.

Punishment of the Civil Disobedient

As explained above, for the purpose of this paper I have construed the civil disobedient as one who breaks the law in order to encourage or bring about a change in the law, either in the law he breaks or in some other law, where usually the law that it is sought to have changed is that of the protestor's country or of that in which the protest occurs. The civil disobedient may break a law because he thinks that it is a bad law on moral, political, ideological, or economic grounds, or he may break what is a just and useful law in order to focus public attention on some other law which he believes to be in need of reform or repeal. He differs from the conscientious objector, in terms of my account, in that his prime concern is to bring about a change in the law rather than to protect and keep intact his own moral integrity. His moral integrity is involved to the extent that he may feel that whereas obeying the law is not in itself something that it is wrong for him to do, not to protest and disobey either the offending law or a law which is made a symbolic law for purposes of protest is to neglect a duty. Thus the conscientious objector becomes a criminal to protect the very essentials of his moral integrity. The civil disobedient disobeys a law in order to do what he believes he ought to do; for him to abstain is to neglect to do what he sees to be a duty, although not necessarily a stringent duty.

Much of what has been said concerning the conscientious objector criminal applies equally to the civil disobedient in respect of the retributive theory. The major difference is that the need for punishment of civil disobedients may commonly be much greater and more pressing, even in constitutional, liberal, democratic societies. A well-run, just community seeks to reduce to a minimum the number of occasions on which any of its citizens will feel obliged to become conscientious objector criminals; it may move in this direction so far that the inconvenience to the community which comes from not punishing the few citizens who feel obliged to become criminal conscientious objectors may be sufficiently slight as to be such that the community can easily bear it. On the other hand, in communities in which the right of protest is recognized provided it does not involve illegal action, individuals may and do come to extend their protests to illegal defiance of laws. In such communities, the need for punishment to maintain not simply law and order but the very values on which the society is founded and which it is designed to protect and foster may be frequent and great. Frequent illegal protests by civil disobedients may endanger basic values such as individual liberty, respect for persons, justice, happiness, pleasure, privacy, to mention only some values and some rights that may be involved.

The retributive theory seems not to provide a philosophical basis in terms of which the desirable and necessary punishment can be determined and justified. That punishment is seen to be at least sometimes necessary and/or desirable, even when not grounded on considerations of retribution, may suggest that a utilitarian justification is available and appropriate. Again, the considerations which relate to the conscientious objector criminal who is subjected to utilitarian punishment hold here. There is a moral insensitivity, indeed, something akin to an abandoning of morality, in punishing one who is doing what he sincerely, possibly rightly, believes to be obligatory merely because such punishment is useful.

The reason that such punishment is sometimes necessary, desirable, and justified is to be found, not in terms of its utility in the narrow sense of the securing of pleasure, happiness, or certain valued goods but in terms of the maintenance of general values additional to utilitarian values, values such as respect for persons, justice, and human rights generally. A society in which conscientious disobedience and civil disobedience were never penalized, and in which the law sought to avoid situations ever arising in which there would be conscientious objectors and civil disobedients to any laws would be one which failed to uphold the very values upon which the retributive theory of justice in punishment is based, namely, the values of respect for persons and for justice. The conscientious objector criminal, often in acting conscientiously and showing respect to himself as a person, shows lack of respect for others as persons, as well as acting unjustly towards them. So too with civil disobedients. In recent years we in the Western World have had the spectacle of self-righteous minorities imposing their wills and their highly dubious views of justice on majorities in coercive ways which involve injustices to many and lack of respect for their opponents as morally autonomous persons. Civil disobedience in particular is commonly a means of using illegal force to coerce others into doing or accepting what they believe they ought not to accept. It may be justified, and justified in terms of justice and respect for persons. Equally, depending on the laws and the causes involved, it may be unjustified and evil. In any event, any state which is concerned with maintaining such values as are prized in a liberal society: liberty, egalitarian justice, fraternity, pleasure, happiness, self-development, respect for persons as persons, cannot abdicate the right to use punishment and force for purposes of social control. The justification of such punishment, when it is justified, is in terms of its necessity for social control to realize and uphold some or all of these values, but in such a way that desert is a relevant, *prima facie* consideration when it figures in the situation. Such a justification of punishment is not a utilitarian one, but one in terms of a wide range of values which include but go far beyond and which may conflict with those acknowledged even by ideal utilitarians. Such punishment for the sake of the values to be secured by social control may be likened to the use of penalties in games, where the penalties maintain the game and the ends of the game. Without the imposition of penalties for breaking the rules — for cheating, even cheating from the highest motives — the game and the ends of the game would cease to be possible. If the game and its ends are worthwhile, the penalties are justified. This general point can be developed further by considering punishment for political offenses and for that wide rage of crimes covered under the general description of "contempt of court." First, however, we might briefly note one important sub-class of moral crimes, namely, those committed against or in defiance of industrial laws on moral grounds.

Industrial Moral Crimes

Industrial laws which render strikes and lock-outs crimes are commonly infringed from reasons of self-interest. However, they may also be broken from a sense of injustice, in order to realize justice. The moral law-breaker who thereby renders himself a criminal is then subject to punishment. The punishment often takes the form of fining the union responsible for the strike, and, if the fines are not paid and the money cannot be obtained from the unions by other means, the leaders may be imprisoned. They may even be held in contempt of court and imprisoned for an indefinite period, i.e., until they purge their contempt or until the court exercises its discretion. What is the justification of such punishment? A consideration of the history of the nineteenth century industrial laws in capitalist societies reveals that very often individuals were rendered criminals for demanding what was not simply what was claimed to be just, but what is now seen plainly to have been just. Again, in so far as a justification is possible, and obviously some control of industrial relations and actions in industry between employer, employee, and the community is necessary, the justification must be in terms of the need for some social controls to maintain, uphold, protect, and realize certain values, including those of the welfare of the community, the consumer, the worker and the employer, such that justice is achieved and respect for all as persons is shown. The lack of justification of much actual punishment springs from the fact that the laws, and the punishment which backs the laws, impede and frustrate the realization of important values for the sake of which we accept social controls when they are justified. To repudiate this punishment is to repudiate the laws from which it springs.

Political Crimes

Political crimes here are interpreted as crimes committed not simply for political reasons by civil disobedients, but by revolutionaries who seek not the repeal or modification of this or that law, but either the abolition or reconstruction of the state as a whole. Obviously whether the state is justified in punishing such political offenders depends on the values they threaten and those they seek and can reasonably hope to realize. Thus again the cases for and against punishment revolve around the values secured or thwarted by the social controls of punishment.

Punishment for the Offense 'Contempt of Court'

Some of the most morally repugnant punishments imposed under the British system of justice are punishments for what is called "contempt of court," this descripiton covering a wide range of offenses. Sentences imposed for contempt of court are commonly indeterminate, and are terminated at the judge's discretion or as a result of the individual purging his contempt by making an apology or entering into undertakings not to act in certain ways. Usually those punished for the offense of contempt of court are not acting from a concern to do their duty — they may act from anger, rashly insulting the judge; they may act in the hope of making a financial gain as in publishing sensational material which increases the sales of their newspapers at the cost of possibly causing an unfair trial; they may simply act in ignorance, or from stupidity; they may act from criminal motives with the intention of bringing about a miscarriage of justice. However, there are cases in which individuals deliberately commit the offenses of contempt of court from a sense of duty because they believe that they morally must do or say that which will render them criminals, guilty of contempt of court in order that justice and good may prevail. Three examples will suffice here. A court may order a husband never to visit his wife and children. The husband knows that his wife is unfit to rear his children, that it is because of perjured evidence that the court made its decision, and that he is in duty bound as father of his children to see them as often as he can in order to instruct them in the right way to order their lives. He disobeys the court order and is imprisoned for an indeterminate period, until he undertakes never to visit his children. This he refuses to do because he will not renounce his duty. A second case is that of the wealthy person who rightly believes that justice is not being done to a group of deformed children whose deformity has resulted from the negligence of a drug company in releasing for sale without warnings to the general public, including pregnant women, a drug which brings about deformities in the foetus. The drug company uses the law, which in essentials is a just system of rules, to evade its responsibilities. The wealthy man, in defiance of the court, uses an opportunity in a TV interview to give the history of the case and his assessment of what would be just action and compensation by the drug company. He also circulates pamphlets to this effect and refuses to promise to desist from such activities. He is jailed for contempt of court but pays various of his distinquished employees to continue with such activities, this being known to the court. He is severely punished. He cannot appeal. He does what he does out of respect for justice and for persons. His desert would seem obviously to be reward, not such punishment as deserved retributive punishment. A third case is that of a person who believes Roman Catholicism to be a heathenish religion and who, when Mass is being celebrated, uses a loud-speaker car to proclaim his belief outside as many Roman Catholic churches as he can. Prosecution as a disturber of the peace and for offensive behavior fails to deter him, so a court order is issued restraining him from such conduct. This he ignores and as a result he is imprisoned for contempt of court. He breaks the law from a concern to do what he religiously and morally believes to be right and obligatory. Again it may well be asked: "What, in terms of the retributive theory, are his deserts, what does he deserve to receive for his actions?" Can meaning be given here to legal desert, as distinct from moral desert, in a relevant way? The utilitarian account of punishment can deal more plausibly with this latter case than with the former two cases.

The justification of that punishment which results from rendering contempt of court a crime of those who for selfish or other non-moral reasons disrupt the running of a just legal system is again to be found in terms of the need of a system of penalties designed to secure the efficient operation of the legal system. The punishment is justified, when justified, because it is useful, not in the narrow utilitarian sense but in the much more widely embracing sense of contributing to the upholding of basic values, non-utilitarian as well as utilitarian values; and this involves reference to desert. Where the person acts from moral motives, the case for the imposition of the penalty requires special consideration because respect for the values the penalties are designed to protect involves respect for the moral agent who is guilty of contempt of court. To treat all cases of contempt of court alike is a mistake, a mistake all too commonly made.

If punishment by the state in these areas is likened to penalties in games designed to sustain the game and the values underlying it, it would then seem that the notion of commensuration, and to a lesser extent that of desert, are neither relevant nor crucial, that the penalty, its nature and severity, should be determined solely by reference to what is necessary to achieve the object sought. Yet part of what shocks one in respect of punishment for contempt of court, in particular, and punishments justified in terms of the need of social control to maintain a desired kind of social order, is that they may be very severe, indeed, grossly excessive, and in no way commensurate with what is deserved. Indeed, it shocks that some such uses of organized force by the state are called punishments rather than simply preventions, internments, quarantinings, or the like. That is to say, even if it be acknowledged that the justification of certain punishment by the state, including that of "moral criminals," is to be found in terms of penalties necessary for social control directed at realizing and maintaining a society in which certain basic values are realized, the notions of desert and commensuration cannot entirely be set aside. Guilt is an essential condition, but commensuration also enters into the notion of desert, even though there are obvious difficulties in spelling out how desert in such punishments is to be determined, assessed, and weighed against the other relevant values. This is a large part of the problem of explaining and justifying as just and morally justified that punishment by the state which is not fully to be justified *solely* in terms of the retributive theory. For reasons I have indicated elsewhere, the retributive theory is seen to be the core to any satisfactory account of the bulk of justifiable punishment by the state.

HUGO ADAM BEDAU
A World Without Punishment?

Today, in contrast to whatever may have been true in earlier, more complacent times, current modes of punishment and the criminal justice system which prevails in our society have become the object of various familiar objections.[1]

(1) Too many classes of acts (e.g., gambling) and conditions (e.g., public nudity or drunkeness) are punishable offenses; we suffer from an acute case of "overcriminalization."

(2) Too few of those who are guilty of dangerous and harmful acts are caught, too few convicted, and too few punished.

(3) Too many people are behind prison bars mainly on account of their class or status rather than as a result of their acts, e.g., they are blacks, or long-hairs, or poor, or all three.

(4) Too many people are sentenced to overly harsh punishments: harsh because severe, e.g., long term imprisonment for possession of marijuana; harsh because vague, e.g., indeterminate sentences for any offense.

(5) Too many people are punished by imprisonment rather than being dealt with alternatively by the criminal justice system, e.g., conscientious draft resisters who during the 1960's were prosecuted and convicted as common criminals rather than treated non-punitively in light of their conscientious motives.

(6) Too many punishments are imposed by statutes which rest on vague grounds of general deterrence and lack empirical evidence to show that such threats are likely to influence the conduct of large numbers of potential offenders.

(7) Too many people suffer from harms and hardships which are not properly part of their punishment but which they cannot escape

once they are at the mercy of those charged with the administration of punishment, e.g., the bail-or-jail system, overcrowded pre-trial detention facilities, abuses by the custodial staff in prison, victimization at the hands of other inmates.

(8) Too many people are simply the victims of official lawlessness inflicted upon them by the corrupt and the vindictive, e.g., police brutality, judicial venality.

(9) Too many people are being made worse by the prevailing system of punishment.

While particular grievances inspire such criticisms, they have led some to mount a radical challenge against the whole system. These grievances have inspired the vision of *a world without punishment*, a utopia long admired by anarchists and socialists, in which not only the whip and the gallows have disappeared, but in which shackles and bars, and all other devices whereby the state enlists coercive force against its own citizens in the name of "law and order," are abandoned. The combined effect of piecemeal objections to punishment can be the dream of a non-punitive, non-repressive society, a true community. This vision is interesting to contemplate if only because it raises some hard questions. Could we in fact entirely abolish all our punitive institutions and practices without utter chaos? What would be the result of such an anti-penal orientation in practice if we left everything else in society the same, e.g., did not simultaneously become hermits or saints, did not pursue radically different social and economic policies, did not confront acute limitations on natural resources? Would the result be a reasonable bargain for everyone, worth paying the costs of no punishment in order to get the advantages of no punishments? If the bargain seems a bad one (as it must to most people), and yet if the particular complaints aired against the prevailing system of punishment are nevertheless true, what modifications might we make either in our theory of punishment or in our penal practice so as to get a better system than we have at present?

The position I defend would answer some of these questions as follows. First, punishment necessarily has some features about it, viz., the deprivation of rights or the imposition of pain, which are bound to make it unattractive to decent persons and also to lend itself to abuses. Second, a fair assessment of current theory as to the nature and justification of punishment shows that the present system of punishment is unintelligible and indefensible. The resulting effects of this assessment upon the theory of punishment are as yet uncalculated. Third, except for fatal and mutilative punishments, whose direct effects are clear, we are not able to predict the total effect upon any given person of subjecting him to a given punishment for a given offense. This should make us extremely cautious about imposing some modes of punishment, e.g., long term detention, upon anyone who is expected subsequently to assume (or resume) a place in society as a normal individual. Fourth, the notorious harms imposed by the existing system of punishment justify immediate experimentation with radical alternatives wherever feasible. Even if abolition of the current penitentiary system of imprisonment is highly desirable, one should not suppose that this can be done without considerable costs and new incentives which may turn out to contradict essential features of our post-industrial society. Fifth, at the present time there is no general alternative available to us and acceptable by the public which is at once superior to punishment in avoiding its harms and abuses and not less effective in response to the genuine problem of criminal violence. Finally, whereas the grievances against the present system of punishment are genuine and legitimate, other considerations show that a world without punishment is both unattainable and undesirable.

It is not possible in brief compass to establish in detail the truth of all these claims, so far stated without even the semblance of argument. However, if we critically examine the current ideas among philosophers as to the nature and justification of punishment, we can see at least how the first three of the above half-dozen claims are correct, and, along the way, add some explanatory support for the other claims as well.

II

During the past twenty years, philosophers in the English-speaking world have reached general agreement as to the nature of punishment. The roots of this conception are at least as old as Hobbes's *Leviathan*[2], but not until fairly recently has the task been undertaken of giving an exact and formal definition of punishment. The task may at first seem quite easy ("Everyone understands what punishment is," says conventional wisdom), but it is not. A formal definition any concept poses certain constraints. In addition, there are many things which are like or concurrent with punishment and thus difficult to distinguish from it, and this will confuse all but the most alert and skillful. For instance, in order to understand the idea of *punishing a person*, it is necessary to distinguish it from such related but different notions as controlling a person's conduct, revenge, intentionally harming another, unintentionally harming another, treatment, blaming, and shaming. Similarly, one must distinguish a person's being punished from a person's being taxed, feeling guilty, being blamed, being hurt. And one must be prepared to say whether God (if there is or were a God) could punish a person, whether a person can punish himself, whether the innocent can be punished, whether a dog can be punished, and so forth. It is out of the attempt to make these distinctions and answer these questions that the current consensus on the nature of punishment has emerged.[3] It can be expressed in the following statement:

A person, P, is punished by something, x, if and only if

(i) x is some pain or other consequence normally considered unpleasant,

(ii) x is intentionally imposed upon P by someone else, Q,

(iii) Q has the authority under the rules of the (legal or other) system to impose x upon P,

(iv) x is imposed on P by Q on account of an offense as defined by the (legal or other) rules,

(v) because P is authoritatively found to be the offender.

For our purposes, the emphasis upon *legal* rules in the above definition is unobjectionable, because in the present discussion, the idea of punishment and its attendant institutions are those of punishment within legal systems (in contrast to the punishment parents visit upon their children, school authorities upon students, etc.). Punishment, of course, is not confined to acts of government under law. Yet it is such punishments which pose the gravest social problem and which are primarily at issue whenever one seriously contemplates the idea of a world without punishment.

Now, if what one wants to do is to attack or criticize the very idea of punishment in order to eliminate the practice or institution of punishment from public life, theoretically the easiest way to do this would be to argue, on some ground or other, that one or more of the five conditions used in this definition has *no* proper application in human affairs. Consider in this light the complaint, mentioned earlier, that we suffer from an acute case of "overcriminalization."[4] The point of this complaint amounts to an attack under clause (iv) in the above definition; "overcriminalization" is the complaint that consensual conduct should not be made a criminal offense, and that we should repeal or nullify all statutes in the penal code which do so. The result would be a vast increase in the amount of conduct which is no longer criminal and therefore no longer punishable as such. In order to attack punishment by the route of pressing the objection of "overcriminalization," a further step must be taken. One must argue either that the conduct in question is not really harmful, or that although it is harmful it must be permitted because it cannot be prevented, or that its harmfulness can be controlled and regulated in non-punitive ways. In a similiar manner, all the classic complaints against punishment can be understood and diagnosed by reference to this definition of punishment.

Before turning to a major objection to punishment as here defined, it is useful to consider first two relatively minor objections. Alternatives to punishment are almost invariably inspired by the feature of punishment identified in clause (i) of the above definition: the infliction of *pain*. Decent people are naturally repelled by the deliberate infliction of pain by one person upon another, except, perhaps, when the person has given his knowing consent to the suffering (as in earlier days, before the development of effective anesthesias, when a gangrenous limb had to be amputated to avoid death). It should be understood, however, that pain — the sensation or the feeling of physical or psychological pain — is neither a necessary nor a sufficient condition of punishment. That it is not a sufficient condition is shown, of course, by the presence of four other conditions in the standard definition of punishment. That it is not a necessary condition, however, is not so readily grasped. Yet consider the death penalty. It is hardly to be denied that killing persons is both a conceivable and an actual mode of punishment. But are we to suppose that it would cease to be a punishment if the sentence of death were carried out by administering (as, supposedly, happened to Socrates when he drank the hemlock) a lethal potion which is *entirely painless?* One might argue that such a painless execution is not as much of a punishment as an agonizingly painful execution; but this hardly matters. What does matter is that by executing a person, one has destroyed his capacity for any future experiences and conduct; one has *deprived* him of his life, something which, presumably, he values (most people do) and to which he has (absent his criminal conduct) a *right.* Accordingly, I would propose that the reference to pain in clause (i) of the standard definition of punishment be revised so as to refer instead to the deprivation of a person's rights.[5] A punishment, especially a punishment under law, always deprives a person of something to which he normally has a right, e.g., his life (the death penalty), his liberty (prison), or his property (fines). Whether or not he minds this, whether or not it also hurts him in some ordinary sense, is incidental. He has lost something of value, whatever he thinks or feels about it; and to do that to a person, in conformity with the other features of the concept of punishment outlined above, is to have punished him. Incidentally, it is just this feature of the revision of clause (i) above which helps us to see what it is about "enforced treatment," such as the regimen of "behavior modification" displayed in Anthony Burgess's *A Clockwork Orange,* which explains why one feels that the society therein depicted has not really abandoned punishment for therapy, but merely exchanged one mode of punishment for another. What remains constant in both cases, as the novel (and movie) show, is the deprivation of offenders' rights by duly constituted authority in consequence of the violation of the criminal code. And that is punishment, whatever else we may choose to call it.

The second preliminary objection is concerned with what we are to infer from our definition of punishment as to the *point* of punishing people. Even though, under this definition, punishing a person is an *intentional* undertaking, it is not clear *what* the intention is with which, in general, we punish people at all. To clarify the problem, consider what a judge should say to a typical burglar when sentencing him to three years in the penitentiary. If the judge is persuaded by our definition of punishment, he might say, "By the authority vested in me, I hereby sentence you to three years in the penitentiary *because* of your conviction on the offense as charged and the statutes providing such punishment for burglary." But what should the judge say if he begins in this way: "By the authority, etc., three years in the penitentiary *in order* to . . . ?" In order to *what?* In order to prevent him from any further burglary during the next three years? In order to make the burglar less inclined to further burglary after the next three years? In order to discourage other would-be burglars? In order to make the convict worse off, as cynics and the recidivism statistics would indicate? The definition of punishment under consideration gives no single answer to this question, and the issue before us is whether this is a merit or defect in the definition, or neither.

Some theorists think it is a defect, because when they define punishment, they do not leave open this question of point in punishment. Thus, Herbert Packer defines (he says "describes") punishment as "all the ways of dealing with people that are marked by . . . a dominant purpose that is neither to compensate someone injured by the offense nor to better the offender's condition but to prevent further offenses or to inflict what is thought to be deserved pain on the offender."[6] Similarly, Joel Feinberg has said that the standard definition of punishment "seems to many to leave out . . . altogether the very element that makes punishment theoretically puzzling and morally disquieting."[7] What is that "element"? Feinberg answers that it is the point, or purpose, or aim of the institution of punishment itself: "the expression of attitudes of resentment and indignation, and of judgments of disapproval and reprobation [toward the offender], on the part either of the punishing authority himself or of those 'in whose name' the punishment is inflicted."[8] Notice that, although Packer and Feinberg agree in objecting to our definition of punishment, they disagree over the presumed intention with which society punishes. But is either of their criticisms correct?

Feinberg's is certainly the more plausible. What Packer calls "the dominate purpose" of punishment and would therefore incorporate *within* the nature and definition of punishment is what many theorists would, rightly, I think, regard as part of its *justification* and therefore as something *external* to the definition. To accept Packer's account of the purpose of punishment forecloses the justification of punishment by deterrence ("to prevent further offenses") and retribution ("to inflict what is thought to be deserved pain on the offender"). But once this is done, what is there left to appeal to as the justification of punishment? Furthermore, it would seem impossible, on Packer's view, to claim to have punished someone and yet not to have tried (and succeeded?) either to prevent further offenses or to cause deserved pain. Yet this does not seem self-contradictory or unintelligible at all; in fact, it often happens. The "expressive function" of punishment, however, does seem at least internal to the nature of punishment and thus a feature of every act of punishing someone. How could we punish a person and fail to express our condemnation of his unlawful conduct? If, therefore, it seems outrageous to suppose that there is no answer to our hypothetical question posed earlier ("An offender is punished 'in order to' — what?"), the proper way for the judge to speak to the guilty is to say in effect, "We sentence you to three years in the penitentiary *in order to* express society's condemnation of your felonious deed." All further purposes, particularly of deterrence and prevention, can be left to the justification of punishment. They need not be built into the very concept of punishment itself.

Yet, plausible as this is, it may still be in error. Why *must* there be any general intention with which society punishes its deviant and dangerous members? Why *must* there be some one thing (or, for that matter, some two or three things) which we do when we punish? A stray remark of Wittgenstein's anticipates these hesitations:

> 'Why do we punish criminals? Is it from a desire for revenge? Is it in order to prevent a repetition of the crime?' And so on. The truth is there is no one reason. There is the institution of punishing criminals. Different people support this for different reasons, and for different reasons in different cases and at different times . . . And so punishments are carried out.[9]

Wittgenstein has not given an argument for the view that there is no single "in order to" about punishment. All he has done is help us to see that, in believing there is some one "in order to," we are ourselves in the grip of a certain picture about the institution of punishment under law, a picture for which we lack adequate evidence, a picture *not necessary*. Even if he is in error and views such as Feinberg's (or even Packer's) are correct, it still remains true that the motives, intentions, purposes, aims or goals of punishment are to some extent hidden from view and to some extent simply fictions derived from imputing to society notions (such as intentions, etc.) which have exact and literal reference only to particular individuals. If the standard definition of punishment leaves the institution of punishment an ambiguously (or vacuously) purposive practice, that may be a mark in favor of the definition. Of course, it may also provoke challenges to the idea of an institution as pervasive and as painful as punishment which lacks any central purpose. In any case, since there is no way for society (or the legislature, or even the judiciary) to say what its intentions are in preserving the institution of punishment, it is extremely difficult to see how we can hope to resolve this dispute either way.

Notice, finally, how natural it is, if we follow the standard conception of punishment, to exclude from a person's punishment all those things which he finds unpleasant, harmful, degrading, or a rights deprivation and which are also distinguishable from the things of this sort to which he was *sentenced* by someone having the authority to impose such deprivations on him. The standard conception of punishment encourgages us to identify as a person's punishment for burglary, say, only and exactly the three years in prison to which he was sentenced by a judge for that crime.

The reality of prison life, however, suggests that this conception is amiss. The quality of life which the typical prisoner experiences in the typical prison while serving his sentence is not adequately conveyed in the phrase, "three years in prison," even though in theory it is that phrase which denotes the entirety of his punishment. There is a vast range of deprivations and harms, indiginities and inconveniences, injuries and terrors, which typically afflict the prisoner during his imprisonment. The *Attica* report and other recent prison documents amply establish this point in convincing detail.[10] No one can read this literature without a shudder at the thought of spending several years in such a place. But of such deprivations there is no allusion whatever in the prisoner's sentence itself. Are they, therefore, to be regarded as incidental aggravations, as theoretically irrelevant abuses of the penal system, and thus as defects of the system of actual punishment but not actually defects in penal theory and the concept of punishment?

We have here, I suggest, a glimpse of the most significant reason why there is practical relevance in a firm grasp of conceptual matters. It is only by relying on a fixed and trustworthy conception of what punishment is that we can proceed to understand the sort of criticism which it is appropriate to make of a given deprivation inflicted upon a person in the name of punishment. Some deprivations, as we have seen, are inseparable from the idea of punishment, but others are separable in theory and perhaps in practice as well. The problem is that many of the theoretically incidental aggravations of punishment in prison are widespread, long-standing, predictable, and beyond the power of most reformers to uproot. Moreover, as the *Attica* report and related documents show, it is often these seemingly incidental aggravations which the prisoner feels most acutely during his term of imprisonment, no matter what the sentencing authority, the general public, or philosophers fixed upon a narrower conception of punishment may think.

There are really only two ways to respond to this gap between theory and practice. One way is to accept it and to try to understand and remove aggravations endemic to actual prison life but ancillary to the necessary deprivations of punishment. The other way is to alter our definition of punishment so as to take these aggravations into account in a systematic, theoretical way as components of the true nature of punishment through imprisonment. At the present time, the pattern of arguments made by prison reform spokesmen is noticeably in favor of the former alternative.[11] According to most reformers, punishment does not require the miseries which imprisonment makes inevitable. Short of abandoning the idea of punishment itself as something unworthy of institutionalized practice, we must press for greater separation between unnecessary deprivation and punishment. We cannot even begin to think through this distinction without an adequate grasp of the idea of punishment itself. The standard conception of punishment, revised perhaps in the directions discussed earlier, goes a long way toward satisfying that need.[12]

III

Textbooks and treatises inform us that there are fundamentally three justifications of punishment: Retribution, Prevention (or Deterrence), and Reformation (or Rehabilitation).[13] Actually, the truly traditional justifications have been only the first two. Because I intend here to concentrate on them exclusively, it is best to say a brief word now about what is wrong with reformation or rehabilitation as the justification of punishment, which came into prominence only during the past century. Rarely has reformation or rehabilitation been held to be the *sole* or event the *primary* justification of punishment. Those who conceive of a world without punishment, and are thus ready to condemn all punishment for anyone no matter what the offender has done, do not have rehabilitation or reformation of offenders in mind when they do so. On the contrary, they often want to get rid of "punishment" in order to rehabilitate offenders. What they condemn is the abuse or neglect of the rehabilitative ideal. In other words, today, reformation or rehabilitation as the goal, aim, or justification of punishment has become progressively blurred with a *non-punitive alternative* to punishment, i.e., Treatment or Therapy.[14] This is but one result of viewing crime less as an example of individual wickedness and more as an instance of social sickness (as is neatly conveyed in the quip from *West Side Story*, "He's depraved on account of he's deprived"). For these reasons we can afford to omit any further canvass of punishment as rehabilitative in this discussion.

Before we can come to grips with the traditional justifications, we need to make an important distinction as to what it is those justifications purport to justify. There are two possibilities. Is it to try to justify the punishment meted out to a given offender for a particular offense? Penal statutes and prison and parole regulations, actual judicial and administrative tribunals, are set up to deal precisely with this task. It is their responsibility not to set general policy but to apply it in individual cases. If that is so, then the justification of any given punishment in an individual case must be entirely a function of two things — the facts in the particular case on the one side and the general rules or policies on the other side. But if that is so, there is nothing more in general to be said about the justification of punishment in individual cases, except possibly to attack this whole approach by arguing for the abandonment of rules, systems, practices, and their institutional counterpart in boards, tribunals, and officers whose task is to administer justice under the rules. Sometimes it does appear as if such an approach were being repudiated by those who preach "individualized" punishment. Actually, however, what is under attack is more likely to be the prevailing system of rules, a system which leaves little room for discretion (and then most of it only to judges in sentencing). What is favored instead is a system which provides a great deal of discretion, most of it allotted to psychiatrists and social workers who deal with the offender after sentencing. The issue, therefore, is not between rules and no rules, but between two different systems of rules. Those on either side of this dispute tacitly agree that what justifies punishment (or treatment) in any given case are the facts of that case and the general policies which apply to it. The true alternative to a system of punishment based on rules is not "individualization" but impulsive and arbitrary responses to individual cases. It is a mistake to suppose that a defense of rules or general policies commits one to a defense of rigid, exceptionless, and unchangeable rules. It is equally a mistake to suppose that the way to improve on bad rules is by abandoning all rules. Consequently, I shall assume henceforth that the only issue before us is one of justifying the system, practice, or institution of punishment in general.

This is particularly important because of the objection often made against Utilitarianism, that it would justify punishing the innocent in some cases, indeed, in all cases where there would be greater social good than harm from such an undertaking. Any system of punishment will have to put up with (that is, excuse) occasional miscarriages of punitive justice. Human frailty guarantees judicial miscarriages, just as it guarantees deliberate occasional abuses of the penal (and all other) institutions of society. By a miscarriage of punitive justice, I mean a case where the person found guilty of a criminal offense and accordingly punished for it was, in fact, not guilty even though he was believed to be guilty by those with the authority to determine guilt and innocence. (I ignore here the problem of a person who is guilty but who, through a miscarriage of justice, is punished more severely than he deserves.) The objection to Utilitarianism is that it allows not only judicial miscarriages but systematic use of scapegoats. Scapegoating — a practice which would allow persons not even believed to be guilty to be processed by the courts as though they were — is not a specially outrageous system of punishment, possibly justifiable on Utilitarian grounds. It is not a form or a part of a system of punitive justice at all! It is, rather, a system of legally sanctioned injury administered in the name of the public whereby innocent victims are framed and the innocent public duped. Neither Utilitarianism nor any other social philosophy could hope to justify or permit such a system.[15] We may fail to realize this so long as we do not distinguish between a system or practice of punishment as such and a particular instance or application of that practice through which each punitive act acquires its own particular nature and character. Justifying a practice, parasitic on true punishment, of systematic scapegoating is one thing; excusing a particular miscarriage of justice within a genuine system of punishment is another. The former would never be justifiable, the latter is all but inevitable.

Let us turn now to the justification of punishment through appeal to retribution. Conceptually, punishment is retributive, as we have seen. There is general agreement that what we mean by punishment is the infliction of some deprivation on someone on account of his infraction of some rule. Retribution therefore enters into the very concept of punishment in a double sense. First, it is retribution which tells us *what* to do in order to punish: "Pay him back in the same coin." Punishment, unlike restitution and compensation to the victims of crime, leaves the person punished worse off than before because the coin in which he is paid back is a deprivation of his rights. Second, it is retribution which tells us *whom* to punish: "The guilty deserve to be punished" is a retributivist tautology. (This, by the way, shows us something peculiar about the very idea of punishing hostages in wartime. Punishment normally requires an identity between the person who is believed to be guilty of an offense and the person punished for it, whereas the practice of punishing hostages deliberately breaks this requirement. Perhaps the phrase, "punishing hostages" is a misnomer.) I see nothing wrong with these two retributivist features of punishment, and I cannot see anything in our institutions of punishment which would be improved systematically abandoning either of these requirements. The fact that there may be more useful, non-retributive ways of handling criminals than punishing them is not an argument for a notion of non-retributive punishment.

Retribution is also often thought to give us possible, even if not necessary, answers to two other questions: Why in general ought we to punish anyone? What in general ought to be a person's punishment for a given offense? The familiar retributivist maxim, "Let the punishment fit the crime," is a partial answer to the second question, and (as is well known) is of little use to us except at the margins. Thus, this maxim assures us that a slap on the wrist for murder is an improper punishment, given the gravity of the offense and the triviality of the punishment. Likewise, death for over-parking suffers from the converse flaw. The problem is to go beyond these margins, and the difficulty for the retributivist lies in showing us *how* we are to assess the relative gravity of other crimes, e.g., rape, kiting checks, and *what* constitutes proportionate severity in punishment for the gravity of each type of offense. But that is not all. Pure retributivism also requires us to be persuaded that no non-retributive considerations should enter into fitting punishments to crimes and to criminals, and that no non-retributive theory has any rational basis for apportioning the severity of punishments to the gravity of offenses. These are strong claims, and, because no version of pure retributivism has made them good, retributivism has been held for some years in low esteem.[16] As to why in general we ought to punish anyone, retributivism seems to be capable of nothing more than the unhelpful circular answer "Because people who commit crimes deserve to be punished." If we ask the retributivist, "Why, in general, do criminals deserve punishment?", either he gives us no answer at all, or he abandons pure retributivism by telling us about the *good on balance* which a system of punishment produces. But this is an ill-disguised, quasi-Utilitarian account of the justification of punishment, and whereas it may be acceptable in its own right, it is not a type of justification open to the pure retributivist.

The only other alternative for the retributivist is to appeal to the idea that *justice* requires punishment of offenders, and that the good which punishment achieves is the good of justice. Sometimes it has even been claimed that punishment is in general *a good to those punished,* irrespective of the overall good to society of having offenders punished. If this is correct, and if this good cannot be obtained in any other way than by punishing offenders, then we have a very strong argument from the moral point of view (the only point of view worth considering on this issue) against a world without punishment. The position has been argued mainly by philosophers influenced by Kant; its most important defense in recent years has been by Herbert Morris.[17] Essential to Morris's restatement of the Kantian theme is the idea that in the typical case it is only by punishing a guilty person that we treat him as a person. "We treat a human being as a person," according to Morris, "provided: first, we permit the person to make the choices that will determine punishment happens to him and, second, when our responses to the person are responses respecting the person's choices."[18] Crucial in the application of these unexceptionable principles to the idea that punishment is a good to persons punished is the belief that in committing a crime a person acts on his deliberate choices and knows that in committing a crime he makes himself liable to some punishment or other.

The chief objection which one might make to this view is quite simple. It would be absurd to imply (as Morris does not) that it follows from the above argument that offenders have a right to be punished by *existing* systems of imprisonment, or that to punish a person in an Attica or a Folsom is to do him some good. Even if a person has the right to be punished, and if deserved punishment does a person good, the offender still has the right to be free of the kind of abuse which existing systems of imprisonment typically impose on him.[19] What makes the very ideas of a right to be punished and of the good of being punished so difficult to accept is their apparent incompatibility with the rights not to be punished in certain way and not to be abused in the name of punishment, and with the harm which actual imprisonment does. These Kantian themes in punishment are somewhat more palatable, I believe, if it is realized that they are advanced (as in Morris's case) in order to offset the undeserved influence of the therapeutic alternative to punishment, which requires us to regard persons who commit crime not as free agents but as sick and helpless. A world without punishment, unless it is also a world without crime, a world without the unjustified violation of the rights of individuals, is certain to be a world with coercion and restraint just the same, with "hospitals" substituted for prisons, "therapists" replacing prison guards, and so on. The net result may be a greater loss of human dignity, as many have argued.[20] The solution here is not (*pace* Austin) any frying pan in a fire; it is to avoid both the freedom-restrictive and rights-violative character of mental and penal institutions as we currently know them.

Is it, then, the retributivist features of punishment which in particular deserve the objections of reformers and visionary critics? I think not, or not mainly, if by this term we mean only the doctrines endorsed so far. We have seen how: (a) punishment involves depriving a person of some of his normal rights; (b) such a deprivation may be visited only upon the guilty (or those authoritatively found to be guilty); (c) the gravity of the offense must to some degree be reflected in the severity of the punishment; and (d) it is not proper to treat a person who deliberately chose to commit a crime as though he were a helpless infant, imbecile, or non-person. It is difficult to see how the institution of punishment could be improved (either in our understanding of it or in its function) by contradicting any of these four principles. Rather, the very reverse of humanization and liberation would result. To abandon these principles is either to make punishment more savage than it already is or to abandon punishment altogether in favor of some more savage alternative. To concede this much in no way requires endorsing any further retributivist principles, whatever they may be. Retributivism no doubt encompasses a variety of principles and notions, but there is no reason why we shouldn't pick and choose among them, retaining only those which fit together rationally with each other and with non-retributive considerations. To the degree to which this is done, the attack upon punishment because of its retributive features should diminish.

Let us turn now to deterrence. There is some confusion as to the nature of deterrence, and since deterrence is the aim or justification of punishment which has become most prominent in our civilization, it is important to clarify this concept at the start. Punishment is generally favored as a systematic way of dealing with offenders because it is believed that punishment prevents crime. But crime prevention as such and prevention by deterrence are two different things. Deterrence, as its etymology suggests, consists in control or influence over the behavior of someone by a *threat*, including the threat of penal sanction. Prevention, however, can be accomplished by any number of methods. For instance, crime can be prevented by manipulating the offender's external environment, e.g., through placing him in prison or stocks, or by banishment. It can be accomplished by alteration of his bodily capacities, through incapacitative and irreversible acts (death, mutilation), or by more subtle and temporary methods (drugs, chemotherapy). Theoretically, all of these are ways of preventing persons from behaving in certain ways and thus from committing criminal acts. *None involves deterrence at all.*

The idea of punishment as a deterrent is complex. Even if prevention is kept distinct from the narrower issue of deterrence, there still remains the further distinction between what is called *special* and what is called *general* deterrence. Special deterrence is usually defined as deterring person A from committing a crime by punishing him for some prior offense; general deterrence is usually defined as deterring persons B, C, D . . . from committing a crime by punishing person A for some offense. Yet both of these definitions are ambiguous because they cut across a further distinction. Consider the situation of special deterrence. Theoretically, we could inflict on any given offender, A, who has committed a crime, x, a punishment, P, and obtain either or both of two deterrent effects: one could be the deterrence from another offense of the same sort, x^1, and another could be the deterrence from an altogether different offense, y (as when, after his release from ten years imprisonment for burglary, Smith is deterred not only from further burglary but also from assault). Let us call the former *primary* deterrence and the latter *secondary* deterrence. The same distinction applies within general deterrence. We have, then, four possible combinations of kinds of deterrence: special and general, primary and secondary. One would conjecture that the imposition of any given penalty would be most effective as a special, primary deterrent, and least effective as a general, secondary deterrent (that is, we would be far more likely to deter Smith from further burglary by punishing him for a prior act of burglary than we would be likely to deter Brown and Jones from assault by punishing Smith for burglary).

Since the time of Beccaria and Bentham, the deterrence efficacy of any given punishment has been understood to be a function of at least five presumably independent variables: severity, certainty, celerity, frequency, and publicity (degree of public perception of the liability to and imposition of the sanction). Subsequent analysis has shown that personality differences among potential offenders are also a relevant variable, and that each of the classic five variables is itself a complex of several factors. Crimes, too, vary in their nature, from the "expressive" — those which evince an inner drive or compulsion and in which prudential self-interest of the offender enters little or not at all — to the "instrumental."[21] It is easy to say, as one of the leading theoreticians of punitive deterrence has written, that "It is . . . a fundamental fact of social life that the risk of unpleasant consequences is a very strong motivational factor for most people in most situations."[22] It is another thing to verify quantitatively its many corollaries. What is the *degree of risk* that persons are willing to run of incurring the legally designated sanction? How *strong a motivational factor* is apprehension of this risk, and on what does its strength depend? How *large a role* does the legal sanction in the narrowest sense — the punishment meted out to an offender by a judge under a statute — play in these "unpleasant consequences?" The truth is, we have almost no reliable answers to these questions, for any given class of offenders, offenses, and sanctions.

Consider, as an example, the ongoing controversy over the relative effect of *severity* and *certainty* of sanctions in deterrence. Classic doctrine would maintain that these two factors are additive, but like much other conventional wisdom this assertion has been attacked. Some have argued that, at least where severe penalties are involved, the two are inversely related (the greater the severity of a sentence, the less certain its application, and conversely). Part of the problem is to determine which statistical model is the best to use in testing these hypotheses. Another part is conceptual: what is the best way to define "certainty" and "severity" in a punishment? Much of the problem lies in the available data on offenses, arrests, prison admissions, and release records. The most recent review of the whole set of issues leaves all of these questions essentially unanswered.[23] This ignorance should make us cautious in the face of the popular maxim, "The greater the severity of a punishment, the greater its deterrent efficacy." In the present state of our knowledge, we have little or no reason to believe that by increasing the severity of a punishment we can achieve a downturn in the crime index, or that by decreasing the severity we should expect an upsurge in crime. The folly of such ideas lies in the notion that we can leave everything else in society the same and control the rate of crime merely by alterations in sanction severity. It is difficult to think of a more naive approach to crime control.

I have stressed these conceptual complexities and empirical difficulties in our knowledge about deterrence because they affect the role it is reasonable to assign to deterrence in the theory of punishment and its justification. Philosophers of a Utilitarian persuasion, such as Bentham and Mill in the last century, tend to stress the importance of deterrence as the sole or the dominant justification of punishment. It is to be found also in the influential views of H. L. A. Hart, who defends the institution of punishment by appealing to its "beneficial consequences" when compared with alternative systematic ways of dealing with crimes and criminals.[24] The chief beneficial consequence of a system of punishment is in "preventing harmful crime."[25] Since incapacitation of convicted offenders play only a small part in crime prevention, it is deterrence which emerges as the "General Justifying Aim" of punishment (in Hart's phrase).

We have seen how, in anything we could properly call an act or a system of punishment, several undeniably retributive features must be present. Can the same be said for deterrence? We have seen earlier how the very nature of punishment would be shaped by some who would build into it a preventative function, and we have also seen the difficulty in giving a retributive account of why anyone ought to be punished at all (i.e., why have a system of punishment?) In addition, we have seen how small a part in justifying punishment is played by appeal to the reform or rehabilitation of convicted offenders. What, then, is left, except an appeal to deterrence and prevention, "social defense" as some now fashionably call it? A dilemma, however, looms precisely at this point, and it is one perhaps better appreciated by the opponents of punishment (or, at any rate, the opponents of a purely deterrence justification of punishment) than by its advocates. The dilemma is that it is difficult to see how deterrence can justify punishment, when (a) we know so little about the deterrent effects, whether special or general, primary or secondary, and when (b) deterrence requires punishing (that is, inflicting a rights-deprivation upon) a person *now* for something he did in the *past* in order to control someone's *future* conduct. Either we must justify both (a) and (b) or we cannot justify deterrence. But if one maintains that deterrence is a necessary justification of punishment, and if deterrence is unavailable to us in theory, then punishment cannot be justified as a system at all!

The idea that it is a moral outrage to inflict pain on a person now in order to influence his or anyone else's conduct in the future we owe to Kant. Recent attempts to get by Johannes Andenaes[26] and Zimring and Hawkins[27] around Kant's objections are not adequate. Andenaes does not even face the dilemma formulated above, much less resolve it. Instead, he appeals to wholly independent moral considerations of proportionality in severity of sentence to gravity of offense and of equality for all offenders before the law. But these two principles neither support nor flow from the idea of deterrence; the fact that they are not incompatible with it, and indeed may limit its abuses, is hardly to the point. Zimring and Hawkins can only fall back on the argument that, in a society which recognizes the rights and interests of offenders as well as citizens generally, convicted offenders forfeit their right not to be deprived of their rights for the good of others on the assumption that they were initially free to conform their behavior to the requirements of the law.[28] But this argument, instead of justifying the forfeiture of rights for the sake of others, merely shows that such forfeiture is required if we are going to punish persons on grounds of deterrence. Those who favor punishment, and especially punishment as justified by its deterrent effects, confront an embarrassment to their views in this unresolved dilemma over deterrence.

IV

Some years ago John Rawls observed that most people regard punishment as "an acceptable institution. Only a few have rejected punishment entirely," he remarked, and as an afterthought added, "which is rather surprising when one considers all that can be said against it."[29] I have tried to show that the concept of punishment is something against which men naturally rebel, for punishment essentially involves a loss of freedom, of rights, and typically is painful and unpleasant for those who must suffer it. I have also tried to show how it is impossible to encompass under the concept of punishment many of the actual indignities and harms inflicted upon the persons who are punished by imprisonment. There is a considerable gap between what its theory of punishment (its conception and justification) can explain and what our practice reveals is in need of explanation.

Meanwhile, crime — not mere law-breaking, but dangerous and harmful conduct inflicted on persons without their consent — continues to be a prominant feature of our lives. There is no immediate prospect of its disappearance from our midst. So long as crime cannot be abolished, or at least diminished to a tolerable level (whatever that might be), there is no likelihood that the practice of punishment will disappear. To say this is not to defend the existing system of imprisonment. The prison system (jails, penitentiaries, prison farms, half-way houses, juvenile detention centers) touches the lives of more than a million offenders every year in this country. It was not built in a day, and it will not be dismantled in a day, not by administrative directive from above, nor by scholarly critique from outside, and not even by riot or rebellion from within. As a human institution, punishment has a disgraceful past; it probably does not have a glorious future. Still, punishment under law as a systematic way of dealing with dangerous and harmful conduct may be the least ugly, the least destructive institution available to us. Bad as it is, the alternatives are worse.

NOTES

[1]See, e.g., *Struggle for Justice*, A Report on Crime and Punishment Prepared for the American Friends Service Committee, New York, Hill and Wang, 1971.

[2]Thomas Hobbes, *Leviathan* (1640), Chapter xxviii, reprinted in part in Gertrude Ezorsky, ed., *Philosophical Perspectives on Punishment*, Albany, State University of New York Press, 1972, pp. 3-5.

[3]Writers who have contributed to this consensus include A. G. N. Flew, Stanley I. Benn, and H. L. A. Hart. See especially Hart, "Prolegomena to the Principles of Punishment," *Proceedings of the Aristotelian Society* (1959-60), reprinted in his *Punishment and Responsibility*, New York, Oxford University Press, 1968, pp. 1-27, especially pp. 4-5. My definition is adapted from Hart's with only minor changes.

[4]For discussion, see Norval Morris and Gordon Hawkins, *The Honest Politician's Guide to Crime Control*, University of Chicago Press, 1970, Chapter i; and the Forthcoming book by Godwin Schurs and myself on crimes without victims.

[5]This revision is not original with me. It may be found already in John Rawls, "Two

Concepts of Rules," *The Philosophical Review* (1955), reprinted in H. B. Acton, ed., *The Philosophy of Punishment*, London, Macmillan, 1969, at p. 111, where Rawls says that he proposes to "define" punishment in terms of a person's being "deprived of some of his normal rights."

[6]Herbert L. Packer, *The Limits of the Criminal Sanction*, Stanford University Press, 1968, pp. 33-34.

[7]Joel Feinberg, "The Expressive Function of Punishment," *The Monist* (1965), reprinted in his *Doing and Deserving*, Princeton University Press, 1970, pp. 95-118, at p. 98.

[8]Feinberg, *loc. cit.*

[9]Ludwig Wittgenstein, *Lectures & Conversations on Aesthetics, Psychology & Religious Belief* (ed. Cyril Barrett), Oxford, Basil Blackwell, 1966, p. 50.

[10]See *Attica*, The Official Report of the New York State Special Commission on Attica, New York, Bantam Books, 1972; and *Prison*, Interviews by Leonard J. Berry, New York, Grossman Publishers, 1972.

[11]See, e.g., *A Program For Prison Reform*, The Final Report of the Annual Chief Justice Earl Warren Conference on Advocacy in the United States, June 9-10, 1972, Cambridge, Mass. This report includes three essays: Caleb Foote, "The Sentencing Function;" Gerhard O. W. Mueller, "Imprisonment and Its Alternatives;" and Herman Schwartz, "Prisoners' Rights: Some Hopes and Realities."

[12]See H. A. Bedau, "Penal Theory and Prison Reality Today," *Juris Doctor*, 2 (December 1972), pp. 40-43, where this point is elaborated.

[13]See, e.g., Ted Honderich, *Punishment: The Supposed Justifications*, London, Hutchinson, 1969; Rudolph J. Gerber and Patrick D. McAnany, eds., *Contemporary Punishment* University of Notre Dame Press, 1972; Stanley E. Grupp, ed., *Theories of Punishment* Indiana University Press, 1971; Acton, ed., *cit.*; Packer, *op. cit.*; and Ezorsky, ed., *op. cit.*

[14]See e.g., Karl Menninger, *The Crime and Punishment*, New York, Viking Press, 1969; and Giles Playfair and Derrick Sington, *Crime, Punishment and Cure*, London, Secker & Warburg, 1965. Perhaps the classic modern source for this idea is the essay by George Bernard Shaw, *The Crime Imprisonment*, New York, Philosophical Library, 1946.

[15]*This is a brief and quite incomplete paraphrase of an argument originating with Kurt Baier, "Is Punishment Retributive" and John Rawls, op. cit., both reprinted in Acton, ed., op. cit.*

[16]See H. L. A. Hart, *Punishment and Responsibility* Oxford University Press, 1968, pp. 230 ff.

[17]Herbert Morris, "Persons and Punishment," *The Monist* (1968), reprinted in Grupp, ed., *op. cit.*, pp. 76-101.

[18]*Op. cit.* p. 92.

[19]See, e.g., Herman Schwartz, *op. cit.*; and Philip J. Hirschkop, "The Rights of Prisoners," in Norman Dorsen, ed., *The Rights of Americans*, New York, Pantheon Books, 1971, pp. 451-468.

[20]See, e.g., Francis A. Allen, "Criminal Justice, Legal Values and the Rehabilitative Ideal," reprinted in Grupp, ed., *op. cit.*, pp. 317-330.

[21]Franklin E. Zimring and Gordon J. Hawkins, *Deterrence: The Legal Threat to Crime Control*, University of Chicago Press, 1973, provide by far the best general discussion of all these issues.

[22] Johannes Andenaes, "The Morality of Deterrence," *University of Chicago Law Review*, 37 (1970), pp. 649-664, at p. 664.
[23] William C. Bailey and Ronald W. Smith, "Punishment: Its Severity and Certainty," *Journal of Criminal Law, Criminology and Police Science*, 63 (1972), pp. 530-539.
[24] Hart, *op. cit.*, pp. 8-9.
[25] Hart, *op. cit.*, pp. 235-236.
[26] Andenaes, *op. cit.*
[27] Zimring and Hawkins, *op. cit.*
[28] *Op. cit.*, quoting Hart, *op. cit.*, p. 244.
[29] Rawls, *op. cit.*, p. 106.

BIBLIOGRAPHY

Books

Acton, H. B. (ed.) *The Philosophy of Punishment: A Collection of Papers.* New York: St. Martin's Press, 1969.
Barnes, H. E. and N. K. Teeters (eds.) *New Horizons in Criminology.* Englewood Cliffs, N. J.: Prentice-Hall, 1951.
Bayles, M. (ed.) *Contemporary Utilitarianism.* New York: Doubleday Anchor Books, 1968.
Beccaria, C. *On Crimes and Punishment,* trans. H. Paolucci. Indianapolis: Bobbs-Merrill, 1963.
Bedau, H, (ed). *The Death Penalty in America.* Garden City: Doubleday, 1964. Revised edition, 1967.
Benn, S. I. and R. S. Peters. *Principles of Political Thought.* New York: Collier Books, 1964.
Bentham, Jeremy. *The Principles of Morals and Legislation.* New York: Hafner Publishing Co., 1961.
Brandt, R. *Ethical Theory.* Englewood Cliffs: Prentice-Hall, 1959.
Cooper, D. E. *The Manson Murders, A Philosophical Inquiry.* Cambridge, Mass.: Schenkman Publishing Co., 1974.
Darrow, C. *Crime: Its Cause and Treatment.* New York: Thomas Crowell and Co., 1922.
Ewing, A. C. *The Morality of Punishment.* London: Kegan Paul, 1929.
Ezorsky, G. (ed.) *Philosophical Perspectives on Punishment.* Albany: State University of New York Press, 1972.
Feinberg, J. *Doing and Deserving: Essays in the Theory of Responsibility.* Princeton: Princeton University Press, 1970.
Gerber, J. and P. McAnany. (eds.) *Contemporary Punishment, Views, Explanations and Justifications.* South Bend: University of Notre Dame, 1972.
Glover, J. *Responsibility.* New York: Humanitites Press, 1970.
Hall, Jerome. *General Principles of Criminal Law.* Indianapolis: Bobbs-Merrill, 1960.
Hart, H. L. A. *Punishment and Responsibility.* Oxford: Oxford University Press, 1968.
Honderich, T. *Punishment, Its Supposed Justifications.* New York: Harcourt, Brace and World, 1970.
Menninger, K. *The Crime of Punishment.* New York: Viking Press, 1968.

Morris, N. and C. Howard. *Studies in the Criminal Law*. Oxford: Clarendon Press, 1964.
Packer, H. *Limits of the Criminal Sanction*. Stanford: Stanford University Press, 1968.
Pincoffs, E. *The Rationale of Legal Punishment*. New York: Humanities Press, 1966.
Ross, W. D. *The Right and the Good*. Oxford: Oxford University Press, 1930.
Wooton, B. *Crime and the Criminal Law*. London: Stevens and Sons, Ltd., 1963.

Articles (not included in anthologies listed above)

Bedau, H. "A Social Philosopher Looks at the Death Penalty," *American Journal of Psychiatry*, 123 (1967).
―――. "The Death Penalty as a Deterrent: Argument and Evidence," *Ethics*, 80 (1970).
Benn, S. I. "An Approach to the Problems of Punishment," *Philosophy*, 33 (1958).
Brandt, R. "A Utilitarian Theory of Excuses," *Philosophical Review*, 78 (1969).
Card, C. "On Mercy," *Philosophical Review*, 81 (1972).
Ezorsky, G. "Retributive Justice," *Canadian Journal of Philosophy*, 1 (1972).
Gehringer, R. E. "Punishment and Responsibility," *Journal of Philosophy*, 66 (1969).
Gendin, S. "The Meaning of Punishment," *Philosophy and Phenomenological Research*, 28 (1967).
―――. "A Plausible Theory of Retribution," *Journal of Value Inquiry*, 6 (1972).
―――. "Insanity and Criminal Responsibility," *American Philosophical Quarterly*, 10 (1973).
Goldinger, M. "Punishment, Justice and the Separation of Issues," *Monist*, 49 (1965).
Kaufman, A. "The Reform Theory of Punishment," *Ethics*, 71 (1960).
Lessnoff, M. "Two Justifications of Punishment," *Philosophical Quarterly*, 21 (1971).
Loftsgordon, D. "Present-day British Philosophers on Punishment," *Journal of Philosophy*, 63 (1966).
McCloskey, H. J. "The Complexity of the Concepts of Punishment," *Philosophy*, 37 (1962).
―――. "Utilitarian and Retributive Punishment," *Journal of Philosophy*, 64 (1967).
Morris, H. "Punishment for Thoughts," *Monist*, 49 (1965).
―――. "Persons and Punishment," *Monist*, 52 (1968).
Stern, L. "Deserved Punishment, Deserved Harm and Deserved Blame," *Philosophy*, 45 (1970).
Van den Haag, E. "On Deterrence and the Death Penalty," *Ethics, 78 (1968)*.

2 3 4 5 6 7 8 9–PP–82 81 80 79 78 77 76